A **LEARN TOGETHER** BOOK

Learn the Gospel

DEEPEN YOUR UNDERSTANDING OF AND TRUST IN THE MESSAGE ABOUT JESUS

TONY PAYNE

SYDNEY · YOUNGSTOWN

Matthias Media
(St Matthias Press Ltd ACN 067 558 365)
Email: info@matthiasmedia.com.au
Internet: www.matthiasmedia.com.au
Please visit our website for current postal and telephone contact information.

Matthias Media (USA)
Email: sales@matthiasmedia.com
Internet: www.matthiasmedia.com
Please visit our website for current postal and telephone contact information.

ISBN 978 1 925424 78 2

Cover design and typesetting by Lankshear Design.

Contents

How to make the most of this "Learn Together" book

This is a special kind of book, and not only because it deals with a special subject—the gospel of Jesus Christ. It's a book that's written to be read and discussed and worked through *with other people.*

It's a **Learn Together** book.

In one sense, every book could be a way to learn together. Talking with other people about the books we're reading is one of the joys of life. Other people teach us, sharpen us, and show us the truth in action.

But this book is particularly and deliberately designed to help *a group of people* learn and grow together. That group might be your family or some friends or a Sunday School class or the regular small group of people from your church that you meet with each week. It might even be just one other person with whom you organize to meet, in order to read and learn and grow together.

The way we've put this book together is built on four

fundamental convictions:

1. God's word, the Bible, is the source of our knowledge of God and of ourselves.

2. God has given us each other to teach and encourage and help each other to learn from his word, and to put it into practice.

3. Reading is a wonderful gift from God—one that is uniquely useful for learning certain kinds of things.

4. A *combination* of learning inputs and approaches is the best way to learn. This book contains multiple opportunities to read, to respond by jotting things down, to listen, to watch, to reflect, and to discuss.

Building on these convictions, we've designed this to be a particular kind of book:

- *It contains sections to read aloud with other people* —you can take it in turns to read, or you might like to appoint someone who is particularly good at reading aloud to do most of the reading. Some of these sections of text will be from the Bible itself.

- *It's a book to write in*—we've provided plenty of white space and generous line spacing so that you can underline things in the text that strike you, scribble in the margins, and jot down your own ideas and what you're learning from others.

- *Interaction and discussion are integral*—at numerous points in each chapter you'll notice some numbered questions. This signals a good point to pause and talk about what you've been reading, using the discussion prompts and questions to help you get started. These questions and prompts are there to help; don't feel you have to use them all—the important thing is to talk together, and to help each other learn and grow.

- *It's a book with bonus videos*—we've produced some free bonus videos that you can also use as you work through this book together (you'll find them at **matthiasmedia.com/learnthegospel**). Depending on the circumstances of your group, for example, it might be helpful to watch a video together outlining or illustrating some of the key content (rather than reading aloud together). At various points in each chapter you'll see a little video icon to show where there is a free bonus video that would fit in well at that point. Make good use of the bonus videos *and* the text in this book. If you decide to watch the video together during your group discussion, read over the text later in your own time to solidify the ideas—and vice versa (if you read the text, watch the videos in your own time). Absorbing the key ideas of each chapter in *both* text and audiovisual form maximizes your learning.

My prayer is that this book will be a useful and enjoyable way to do something supremely important and special: *to learn with other people* what it means to know and serve God through Jesus Christ.

1. Why learn the gospel?

Introduction

In any long-term, important project—whether building a house or building a life—it's vital to pay attention to the *foundations*.

If you're a newish Christian and have a lifetime of spiritual building in front of you, now is the time to make sure that your foundations are solid, square, and true.

If you're a more established Christian, it's also really important to get down under the house and check the foundations. They might have shifted or cracked or been attacked by white ants. Or perhaps they weren't laid quite straight in the first place.

And if you wouldn't yet call yourself a Christian but are interested to find out more, there's no better place to start than with the absolute essentials—the foundations of Christianity.

The foundation of Christian faith and life is *the gospel of Jesus Christ*.

In the eight chapters of this **Learn Together** book,

we'll thoroughly inspect that gospel foundation, and we'll make our understanding of it deep and solid and true. We'll learn *the gospel of Jesus Christ* together —understanding each of its parts and how they fit together, and what implications the various facets of the gospel have for our lives.

1. In as few words as possible, write down what you think the "gospel" is.

2. Talk about why you wrote down what you did.

Why learn the gospel?

a. First importance

The Christian gospel is an announcement of great or momentous news—that's what the word "gospel" means. And like any piece of news, the gospel message can be communicated and understood and remembered clearly, or it can be miscommunicated, misunderstood, or forgotten.

The "gospel," in other words, is the kind of thing that can and should be *learned*.

It may not have occurred to you before that the gospel was something that you should *learn*. But the New Testament certainly assumes that it is. When Paul is urging the Ephesians to abandon their former way of living, he says, strikingly: "But that is not the way you *learned Christ!*—assuming that you have heard about him and were taught in him, as the truth is in Jesus" (Eph 4:20-21). In much the same way, Paul reminds the Colossians that when they first heard the word of truth, the gospel, they "*learned* it from Epaphras our beloved fellow servant" (Col 1:7).

In fact, the apostles often write to believers in the New Testament to *remind* them of what the gospel is, to teach it to them again, and to make sure that they understand it deeply and properly.

A classic example is found in 1 Corinthians 15:1-5, where Paul reminds his somewhat chaotic Corinthian friends of the essentials—the things of "first importance" that he preached to them, and that he wants them to hold on to:

> ¹ Now I would remind you, brothers, of the gospel I preached to you, which you received, in which you stand, ² and by which you are being saved, if you

hold fast to the word I preached to you—unless you believed in vain.

³ For I delivered to you as of first importance what I also received: that Christ died for our sins in accordance with the Scriptures, ⁴ that he was buried, that he was raised on the third day in accordance with the Scriptures, ⁵ and that he appeared to Cephas, then to the twelve. (1 Cor 15:1-5)

3. Why do you think Paul wants the Corinthians to know and remember the gospel?

4. What would you say are the *basic elements* of the gospel in this passage?

 ## b. The courier and his message

(Go to **matthiasmedia.com/learnthegospel** *to watch bonus video 1a at this point if you'd prefer to watch and listen to the next section, rather than read aloud. Otherwise, nominate a member of your group to read this next section.)*

Paul talks about his ministry in 1 Corinthians 15 as if he were a courier. He had been given a message, it was his job to deliver it (by preaching), and that's what he'd done. And this message ("the gospel I preached to you") had become the rock and foundation of his hearers' lives.

Now he wants to make sure that they cling to that rock, because like any message or word you receive it's possible to lose your grip on the gospel—to forget or ignore it, to become confused or vague about it, to mis-remember or distort it. And this would be terrible, says Paul to the Corinthians, because the gospel is the message "by which you are being saved, if you hold fast to the word I preached to you—unless you believed in vain" (1 Cor 15:2).

This is perhaps the most fundamental reason to learn the gospel. *It's the message that saves us, like a rock we cling to in a raging sea.* And the way we cling to that message is by knowing it clearly and continuing to trust it wholeheartedly.

Before we leave 1 Corinthians 15, it's worth noticing how Paul summarizes his "gospel" in a nutshell.

Firstly, the gospel is a message *about a king*. That's what the word "Christ" means. It's an Old Testament term meaning the "anointed one" or "kingly ruler" that God promised he would send to rule his chosen people Israel and the whole world. "Christ" isn't Jesus' surname; it's a title—like saying "King Jesus." The gospel is a message about God's long-promised worldwide king.

Secondly, we only know who or what a "Christ" is, and why his death and resurrection are so important, because of the *Old Testament*. Twice Paul says that the gospel is "in accordance with the Scriptures" (which in this context meant the Old Testament Scriptures). The death and resurrection of Jesus the Christ didn't happen randomly or out of the blue. It was the culmination of the long history of God's purposes revealed to Israel, and we can only really understand the gospel against this background.

Thirdly, the basic content of the message is *the death and resurrection of the king*, Jesus Christ. The gospel is the momentous newsflash that Christ died for sins, was buried (i.e. he really did die), was raised on the third day, and was seen by a whole bunch of people (i.e. he really did rise).

Whatever else Christian faith is about—whatever implications it has or other important themes it addresses —these are the things of "first importance": that as a matter of historical truth the man Jesus died for our sins, and he was raised from the dead on the third day to be the king or Christ of all. This is the center of the center; the foundation on which we take our stand and build our Christian lives.

What Paul says here is echoed in different ways all over the New Testament—that the foundation of our Christian lives is the gospel message about Jesus Christ's death for our sins and his resurrection from the dead to be lord of all, in accordance with the Scriptures. This is the message we need to learn, understand thoroughly, and hold fast to.

And that's what the rest of this book will be about.

5. How do the elements of the "nutshell gospel" in 1 Corinthians 15 compare with your own gospel summaries? What do you notice?

c. More good reasons to learn the gospel

When Paul wrote to the Christians at Colossae, who had "learned" the gospel from his good friend Epaphras (Col 1:7), he was very keen that they stick closely to the one, true, original message (just like with the Corinthians). He didn't want them to become captivated by other "gospels" that were doing the rounds and causing trouble (this is what chapter 2 of Colossians is mostly about).

The particular issue in Colossae seemed to be this: *How does someone grow in spirituality and become more godly?*

Here are some excerpts from Paul's letter. As you read them, ask yourself: *How have the Colossians grown as Christians? How does Paul want them to keep growing?*

[3] We always thank God, the Father of our Lord Jesus Christ, when we pray for you, [4] since we heard of your faith in Christ Jesus and of the love that you have for all the saints, [5] because of the hope laid up for you in heaven. Of this you have heard before in the word of the truth, the gospel, [6] which has come to you, as indeed in the whole world it is bearing fruit and increasing—as it also does among you, since the day you heard it and understood the grace of God in truth, [7] just as you learned it from Epaphras our beloved fellow servant. He is a faithful minister of Christ on your behalf [8] and has made known to us your love in the Spirit.

[9] And so, from the day we heard, we have not ceased to pray for you, asking that you may be filled with the knowledge of his will in all spiritual wisdom and understanding, [10] so as to walk in a manner worthy of the Lord, fully pleasing to him: bearing fruit in every good work and increasing in the knowledge of God; [11] being strengthened with all power, according to his glorious might, for all

endurance and patience with joy; [12] giving thanks to the Father, who has qualified you to share in the inheritance of the saints in light. (Col 1:3-12)

[27] To them [God's people, the saints] God chose to make known how great among the Gentiles are the riches of the glory of this mystery, which is Christ in you, the hope of glory. [28] Him we proclaim, warning everyone and teaching everyone with all wisdom, that we may present everyone mature in Christ. [29] For this I toil, struggling with all his energy that he powerfully works within me.

[2:1] For I want you to know how great a struggle I have for you and for those at Laodicea and for all who have not seen me face to face, [2] that their hearts may be encouraged, being knit together in love, to reach all the riches of full assurance of understanding and the knowledge of God's mystery, which is Christ, [3] in whom are hidden all the treasures of wisdom and knowledge. [4] I say this in order that no one may delude you with plausible arguments. [5] For though I am absent in body, yet I am with you in spirit, rejoicing to see your good order and the firmness of your faith in Christ.

[6] Therefore, as you received Christ Jesus the Lord, so walk in him, [7] rooted and built up in him and established in the faith, just as you were taught, abounding in thanksgiving. (Col 1:27-2:7)

6. From these passages, how would you describe Christian growth or maturity? What are its features?

7. How does Christian growth happen? What drives it or causes it?

8. How does this fit with your own experience of Christian growth?

▶ d. The engine of growth and the word that we share

*(Go to **matthiasmedia.com/learnthegospel** to watch bonus video 1b at this point if you'd prefer to watch and listen to the next section, rather than read aloud.)*

It's hard to think of how a tree with deep roots can "walk" and make progress—unless it is one of those mobile trees from *The Lord of the Rings*—but that's what Paul wants the Colossians to do in the passage we've just looked at.

In order to grow and flourish day by day as Christians (to "walk" in Christ), they need to keep strengthening their roots. And those roots are the gospel message that was received and learned and planted within them— the "word of the truth, the gospel," the message about "Christ Jesus the Lord."

In other words, Paul is reminding them that *the gospel is not only what gets you started in the Christian life; it's also the ongoing engine of Christian growth.* That's why Paul's method for producing Christian maturity is simply to keep proclaiming Christ: "Him we proclaim, warning everyone and teaching everyone with all wisdom, that we may present everyone mature in Christ" (Col 1:28).

Don't look elsewhere; don't move on; don't be enticed by fancy alternatives or add-ons. The deep roots that will nourish us and cause us to grow solid and strong as Christians are the roots of the original gospel message that we received and learned.

This, then, is a further compelling reason to learn and know the gospel thoroughly—*it's the source of Christian growth*.

And there's another reason too, which we also see in Colossians. Towards the end of the letter, Paul lifts the Colossians' eyes from their own issues and struggles to the world outside:

> Continue steadfastly in prayer, being watchful in it with thanksgiving. At the same time, pray also for us, that God may open to us a door for the [message],* to declare the mystery of Christ, on account of which I am in prison—that I may make it clear, which is how I ought to speak.
>
> Walk in wisdom toward outsiders, making the best use of the time. Let your [message]* always be gracious, seasoned with salt, so that you may know how you ought to answer each person. (Col 4:2-6)

Did you notice the repeated word "message" with the asterisk next to it? In the original Greek of the passage, this is the same word each time—it's the word *logos*, which is often translated "word" or "message." The message that Paul has been commissioned to preach, and for which he is now in prison, is also a message that belongs to the Colossians and which they talk about with "outsiders" in the midst of everyday life and interaction.

We should learn the gospel really well *so that we can*

share it with others when the opportunity presents itself. A sure test of whether we've really understood something is whether we can explain it simply and clearly to someone else. And the gospel is no different. It needs to be learned in order to be shared.

Sharing the gospel with others won't be the focus of this book—there's a companion volume to this one that is all about that (*Share the Gospel*). But the first and prior step is to learn the gospel really well.

9. Given the reasons we've explored for learning the gospel, what are you looking forward to most from this book? What do you personally hope to gain?

How we'll learn the gospel

We're going to be learning the gospel using an outline called *Two Ways to Live*. For more than 40 years, *Two Ways to Live* has been used and appreciated all over the world as a simple, clear, logical presentation of the key elements of the gospel.

Two Ways to Live has six main points that focus on the death of Christ for sins and his resurrection from the dead, but which also sketch in some of the background ("in accordance with the Scriptures") that enables us to make sense of what Jesus' death and resurrection mean. The six points are:

1. God as the creator and ruler of the world, and of us
2. Humanity as rebels against the good creator
3. The judgment that we deserve because of our rebellion
4. The death of Jesus for our sins
5. The resurrection of Jesus as God's appointed ruler (or Christ)
6. The response that this gospel calls for.

It is important to realize that *Two Ways to Live* itself is an *outline*. It's like a set of bullet points that seeks to capture the key points of the gospel in the shortest, clearest, most memorable way possible.[1]

---

1   You can find the full *Two Ways to Live* outline on the last two pages of this book.

But underneath each of the short, punchy statements that you'll find in *Two Ways to Live* is a deep well of biblical, gospel truth. In the remaining chapters of this book, we'll draw from that well at some depth, clarifying and exploring the meaning of each of the six points and how they fit together, and reflecting on their implications.

We'll also do something that is a bit unusual these days. We're going to learn the short, memorable statements of *Two Ways to Live* off by heart, so that the truths that they summarize are embedded in our minds to be called upon whenever we need them. Depending on your background, this sort of learning might be unfamiliar to you, but it is immensely helpful for planting the truths of the gospel down deep in our minds and hearts.

At the end of each chapter there will be a learning exercise like the one below ("Learn point 1 of *Two Ways to Live*: Creation"). These exercises are intended to help you learn the next main point of the *Two Ways to Live* outline. (Feel free to use the full *Two Ways to Live* outline at the end of this book as an aid to memorization. Keep reading it through. You might like to take a photo on your phone and carry it around with you.)

Before next time

Reflect and pray about what you've learned in this chapter

Look back over this chapter. Make notes in the margin about truths that prompt you to give thanks and pray. Spend some time thanking God and asking him to write these truths in your heart.

If you watched the videos in your group, make sure you read those sections of text—and vice versa (if you read aloud the sections of text, watch the relevant videos).

Learn point 1 of *Two Ways to Live*: Creation

Step 1

Read the statements aloud three times, tracing over the drawing as you do so.

> God is the ruler of the world. *(draw crown)*
> He made the world. *(draw world)*
> He made us to rule his good world, giving
> thanks and honor to him. *(draw humanity)*

Read the Bible verse and transition statement aloud three times.[2]

---

2   A note about the Bible translations used in this book: for the Bible passages that are studied and quoted, we've used the ESV (as we do in most Matthias Media resources). But when learning and quoting the *Two Ways to Live* outline, we've used the NIV because that is the translation used in the outline (it was deemed a more suitable translation for a wider variety of readers in evangelistic contexts). NIV verses are marked with a † symbol.

> You are worthy, our Lord and God, to receive glory and honor and power, for you created all things, and by your will they were created and have their being. (Revelation 4:11)†

This is how God created things to be. But it's fairly obvious that this is not our experience of the world now. What happened?

Step 1a

Without looking at page 24, fill in the blanks in the statements.

> God is _____ of the world.
>
> He _____ the world.
>
> He made us to _____,
>
> giving _____ and _____ to him.

Check your answers, and make any corrections. Read the corrected version of the statements aloud, doing the drawing as you go.

Fill in the blanks in the Bible verse and transition statement.

You are _____, our Lord and God, to receive

_____ and _____ and _____, for you

_____, and by your will they

_____ and _____

_____. (Revelation 4:___)

This is how God _____.

But it's fairly obvious that _____

_____ of the world now. What

_____?

Check your answers, and make any corrections. Read the corrected Bible verse and transition statement aloud.

If possible, wait some time (perhaps even 24 hours) before moving on to step 2.

Step 2

Fill in the blanks in the statements.

God is _____.

He _____.

He made us to _____,

giving _____.

Check your answers, and make any corrections. Read through the corrected version of the statements, doing the drawing as you go.

Without looking at page 26, fill in the blanks in the Bible verse and transition statement.

You are _____ , our _____ , to

_____ and _____ and _____ ,

for you _____ , and _____

_____ and

_____ . (Revelation ___:___)

This is _____

_____ . But it's fairly _____

_____ of the

_____ . What _____ ?

Check your answers, and make any corrections. Read the corrected Bible verse and transition statement aloud.

If possible, wait some time (perhaps even 24 hours) before moving on to step 3.

Step 3

On a blank sheet of paper, write out the statements from memory, and then correct your version.

Read the corrected statements aloud while doing the drawing.

Repeat this process until you can say the statements perfectly while doing the drawing.

On a blank sheet of paper, write out the Bible verse and transition statement, and then make any corrections.

Read the corrected version aloud.

Repeat the process until you can say the Bible verse and transition statement perfectly.

2. Creation

Review

In pairs or triplets, take it in turns to see if you can repeat to each other from memory the three statements of point 1 of *Two Ways to Live*, and reproduce the drawing.

The place to start

As we began to see in chapter 1, the nutshell of the gospel "newsflash" is that Jesus is the crucified and risen Christ (or king) who invites sinners to be forgiven and become obedient subjects of his kingdom. As we look at the gospel presentations of the New Testament, they repeatedly focus on this essential proclamation.

This is basically the message of point 5 of *Two Ways to Live*:

> God raised Jesus to life again as the ruler and judge of the world.
> Jesus has conquered death, now brings forgiveness and new life, and will return in glory.

And so it might be reasonable to ask why we have points 1-4 of *Two Ways to Live*. Why not just go straight to number 5 and tell people the good news?

It wouldn't be wrong to do that!

But what we also repeatedly see in the New Testament is the apostles giving their hearers the *background* or *presuppositions* of the gospel proclamation, so that they can understand what it means. Sometimes (to Jewish audiences) they gave the Old Testament background that pointed to who the Christ would be (as in Acts 2:14-36 and 3:11-26). Sometimes (to Gentile audiences) they went all the way back to God as creator of all things (e.g. Acts 14:15-17, 17:22-31).

Two Ways to Live does much the same thing. It lays down, in a logical order, the key ideas that need to be in place for the climactic announcement of point 5 to make sense to a 21st-century person (who doesn't know the Bible well).

You can see the logic by working *backwards* from the essential gospel announcement of point 5:

- Jesus the risen ruler offers forgiveness to everyone (point 5). But why did he die in the first place? And on what basis does he offer forgiveness?
- He died as a guiltless substitute to take the punishment that sinners like us deserve (point 4). But why are sinners facing death as a punishment?
- We are all under the rightful judgment of God because of our rebellion against him (point 3). But what do you mean by "rebellion against him"?
- We all reject God as our ruler and run our own lives our own way in rebellion against him (point 2). But why can't we do our own thing? Who made God our ruler?
- God is our ruler because he is our creator, and he made us to rule his world under him, giving thanks and honor to him (point 1).

To understand the extraordinary and wonderful news of Jesus' death and resurrection, we have to go right back to the beginning—to the basic relationship between God, as the lord and creator of all things, and us as his creatures.

Point 1 of *Two Ways to Live* summarizes it like this:

> God is the ruler of the world.
> He made the world.
> He made us to rule his good world,
> giving thanks and honor to him.

Let's unpack the profound truths behind these simple statements by looking at some key Bible passages, starting with Genesis 1:

> [26] Then God said, "Let us make man in our image, after our likeness. And let them have dominion over the fish of the sea and over the birds of the heavens and over the livestock and over all the earth and over every creeping thing that creeps on the earth."
>
> [27] So God created man in his own image,
> in the image of God he created him;
> male and female he created them.
>
> [28] And God blessed them. And God said to them, "Be fruitful and multiply and fill the earth and subdue it, and have dominion over the fish of the sea and over the birds of the heavens and over every living thing that moves on the earth"... [31] And God saw everything that he had made, and behold, it was very good. And there was evening and there was morning, the sixth day. (Gen 1:26-28, 31)

1. What do we learn about the nature of God's creation in this passage?

2. What do we learn about the particular nature of humanity?

3. What role does God give humanity within his creation?

Psalm 33:1-9 says:

> [1] Shout for joy in the LORD, O you righteous!
>> Praise befits the upright.
> [2] Give thanks to the LORD with the lyre;
>> make melody to him with the harp of ten strings!
> [3] Sing to him a new song;
>> play skillfully on the strings, with loud shouts.
>
> [4] For the word of the LORD is upright,
>> and all his work is done in faithfulness.
> [5] He loves righteousness and justice;
>> the earth is full of the steadfast love of the LORD.
>
> [6] By the word of the LORD the heavens were made,
>> and by the breath of his mouth all their host.
> [7] He gathers the waters of the sea as a heap;
>> he puts the deeps in storehouses.
>
> [8] Let all the earth fear the LORD;
>> let all the inhabitants of the world stand in awe
>> of him!
> [9] For he spoke, and it came to be;
>> he commanded, and it stood firm.

4. How did God make the world?

5. What is God still doing?

6. What sort of response is appropriate to God's creation and work in the world?

Now let's turn to the other end of the Bible—Revelation 4:9-11:

> [9] And whenever the living creatures give glory and honor and thanks to him who is seated on the throne, who lives forever and ever, [10] the twenty-four elders fall down before him who is seated on the throne and worship him who lives forever and ever. They cast their crowns before the throne, saying,

[11] "Worthy are you, our Lord and God,
　　to receive glory and honor and power,
for you created all things,
　　and by your will they existed and were
　　　created."

7.　What is God worthy to receive?

8.　Why?

9.　From all that we have seen so far, what would you say humanity's stance towards or relationship with God should be?

 **The key concepts**

a. God the maker and ruler

*(Go to **matthiasmedia.com/learnthegospel** to watch bonus video 2a at this point, or read the following text aloud together.)*

The Bible constantly presents God as the creator of all things, without exception. As John 1:3 puts it: "All things were made through him, and without him was not any thing made that was made." God has made and continues to make everything that exists—in detail—down to the child knitted together in the mother's womb (Ps 139:13).

All this creating has a purpose and a value, as Genesis 1 so often repeats: "And God saw that it was good." The world itself, as created by God, is *good*, and it derives this goodness from the character and intentions of the God who made it.

This has enormous implications for what we believe about the world itself. It means that the world—as God's creation—is not evil or anti-spiritual, but good and lovable. It therefore rules out any denial or despising of the physical world, as many religious traditions have done over the centuries.

However, more importantly, the doctrine of creation has massive implications for what we believe about God. *The doctrine of creation demonstrates and establishes God's rule or lordship over all things.* We owe God all honor and glory, not simply because he is bigger and more powerful than us, and not simply because he is so marvelous and holy and good, but because he created all things (as Revelation 4:11 says).

The authority or rule of God over us is not random or arbitrary—like someone who can tell us what to do because they carry a big stick. God is *our* ruler and lord because we are *his* creatures. We belong to him. And as our creator, he provides for us, and sustains us, and rules us.

God's rule of his creation is continual and ongoing. The world is not a natural machine: a giant piece of clockwork that God made and then wound up and set going, but which he doesn't have much to do with anymore. On the contrary, God continues to rule and supervise all things. "The eyes of all look to you, and you give them their food in due season," says Psalm 145:15.

He also rules over *humanity*. We are part of his creation, and he is in complete sovereign control of us, even down to the decisions of our hearts and minds. "The king's heart is a stream of water in the hand of the LORD," says Proverbs 21:1; "he turns it wherever he will."

So God is creator and lord of all. He creates a good world for a good purpose. And that purpose is only finally understood with the coming of Jesus. The New Testament says Christ was not only the agent of God's creation, as the divine Word, but also the *reason* for creation. "All things were created *through* him and *for* him," says Colossians 1:16. God created the world for man; and the ultimate Man for whom it was made, and who now rules it, is Jesus Christ. (But more of that later.)

LEARN THE GOSPEL

This brings us to the other key concept in this first point of *Two Ways to Live*.

b. Humanity as creatures and rulers

As humans, we are not outside the creation or separate from it. God made us, along with everything else, and we are thus under God's authority and rule as his creatures, and dependent upon him for everything. But we also have a special place within creation.

Our special place in creation is captured in the idea of us being made in the *image of God*. What it means exactly for mankind to be in the image of God has been a topic of much debate, but one of the key aspects of it—if not *the* key aspect—is that being in God's image means that *we rule or have dominion over the world, under God*. When we read Genesis 1:26-28, where the phrase "the image of God" first appears, this seems to be the immediate context of what it means to be God's image in the world—mankind is to have dominion, to rule over the world, to fill and subdue it, to be responsible for it. And in this we are like God; we are in his image. (As we will see in points 4 and 5 of *Two Ways to Live*, Jesus came to fulfill this purpose of God—to be the true image of God and the ruler of God's world.)

But humanity was not only created to be God's deputy in the world, ruling his world under his authority; we were also created to be in *right relationship with*

God—that is, to relate to him with honor, obedience and thanksgiving because of who he really is, the God and ruler and creator of all.

Everyone in the world, no matter their culture or religion or ethnicity, wakes up every morning to see a world that demonstrates the divine power and character of the one God who created it. As Paul says in Romans 1, this should lead us to recognize and honor and worship this God for who he is, and to give him thanks (Rom 1:18-25).

Of course, we don't do that. We suppress this truth, and turn away from our creator—but that is the story of point 2 of *Two Ways to Live*: the rebellion of humanity against the rightful rule of our maker and lord.

10. What difference would it make to how we thought about the world and ourselves if there were no creator?

11. How do you feel about the idea of humanity being put in charge of the world?

▶ Alternatives

*(Go to **matthiasmedia.com/learnthegospel** to watch bonus video 2b at this point, or read the following text aloud together.)*

To understand any truth clearly, we need to know how it differs from the alternatives. In each chapter of this book, we'll not only dig down into a key facet of the gospel (and its background), but we'll also explore how the biblical view differs from, and critiques, other common views in our society.

a. Materialism = matter is all there is

"Materialism" is the view that physical matter is the only thing that exists. There is nothing else in the world except atoms and molecules, and there is no God who made any of it.

This is a minority view in most cultures, but it is becoming more common, especially in the West. It says that we're simply here because we're here. Everything that exists has randomly or accidentally formed itself into its current state of complexity and order. The world has no creator, and thus no ruler.

Many people assume that science has proved this to be the case, but it hasn't. Science investigates the *what* and *how* of the world. It explores how the atoms and molecules fit together, what processes cause various things to work or develop in various ways, and so on.

Science can explore the various ingredients that go into a cake, and how it was cooked, but it can't discover *why* the cake was made. Whatever scientists discover about the processes by which the world has come to be, none of it tells us whether God is the creator of every atom, every molecule, and every process that forms and sustains the world and us. This is simply not the kind of knowledge that science is equipped to discover or to disprove.

Many people like to think that science has proved that physical matter is the only thing that exists, because it's an attractive idea at first glance. If there is no creator God, that makes me answerable to no one. However, on further reflection, it is an awful idea, because it renders the world and us valueless and meaningless—because accidents have no value or meaning in themselves. A cake that somehow assembled and cooked itself would be an extraordinary and very unlikely thing. But it would also be a meaningless thing. It would have been made *by* nobody *for* nobody. It would celebrate no one's birthday or wedding. It would have no value. It would simply exist. Manufactured items are valuable and meaningful because their meaning is supplied by their maker.

But, of course, once you have a maker, then you are responsible to the maker.

b. Mysticism = matter is anti-spiritual

Mysticism is almost the opposite of materialism. It believes that the *non-physical world* (the "spiritual" world) is the real and important world, and that the physical world is evil or unspiritual or just unimportant. In some versions of mysticism, the physical world is not even real (e.g. Christian Science and many Eastern religions).

Mysticism in all its forms regards the physical nature of the world as a barrier to knowing God, and so only by denying yourself physical enjoyment, or escaping physical sensation, or even causing yourself physical pain, can you come to know God.

This is the very opposite of the way that the Bible describes the good world that God made. In fact, it is a demonic alternative, according to 1 Timothy 4:1-4. Everything God has created is good, and is to be received with thanksgiving.

c. Deism = God as watchmaker

The third alternative suggests that the world is a machine that runs on its own. It may have been originally made or set up by God, but he doesn't have any significant ongoing involvement.

This is the default belief of many people today. It's not that they don't believe in God at all—they just don't see God as having any real role or work in the world. God may have designed the world and set it in motion, but he doesn't have much relevance anymore. Science can tell us all we need to know about how to live.

Deism is attractive for many non-Christian people, because it acknowledges the existence of God, but handily keeps him at a distance so that we don't have to listen to him or bother with him. He's an absentee god whom you can conveniently ignore.

This is not at all the Bible's view of God's creation and rule of the world. God continues to rule and provide for every aspect of his world. Even when a sparrow falls to the ground, which seems like an everyday "natural" event, the Bible says it only takes place because of the will of the Father (Matt 10:29). Likewise, when God parted the Red Sea it was a great miracle, but he did it using a strong east wind.

God is in control of every aspect of his creation. You don't see God only when the normal processes of creation are suspended or changed; he is at work all the time at every moment.

12. Which of these alternatives do you think you are most likely to believe or be challenged by? Why?

Summing up

The idea of God as creator is fundamental to the Bible, and to the gospel that is at the center of the Bible.

The truth of creation establishes God's relationship with all of the created order, including humanity. As the all-powerful creator of all things, he is the ruler and lord of all, and is therefore worthy to receive glory, honor, and power.

Without the doctrine of creation, we cannot understand who God is, or which "god" we might be talking about. Without creation, we cannot understand why we owe him all honor, thanks, and obedience, and thus why our rebellion against him is so dreadful, and so deserving of judgment.

Further, in seeing that God created humanity, and gave us a special place in creation as rulers of the creation under him, we foreshadow the coming of Jesus as "the last Adam" (1 Cor 15:45), the one who succeeded where Adam and all his descendants failed, the Man who really will rule the world as God's king and bring God's purposes to fulfillment.

But there is much to say before we get to that point. We next have to consider what exactly has gone wrong with us and the world and our relationship with God.

Before next time

Reflect and pray about what you've learned in this chapter

Look back over this chapter. Make notes in the margin about truths that prompt you to give thanks and pray. Spend some time thanking God and asking him to write these truths in your heart.

If you watched the videos in your group, make sure you read those sections of text—and vice versa (if you read aloud the sections of text, watch the relevant videos).

Learn point 2 of *Two Ways to Live*: Sin

Step 1

Read the statements aloud three times, tracing over the drawing as you do so.

> We all reject God as our ruler *(draw large crown and cross it out)* by running our own lives our own way. *(draw small crown and humanity)*
> By rebelling against God's way, we damage ourselves, each other, and the world. *(draw world under large crown)*

Read the Bible verse and transition statement aloud three times.

> We all, like sheep, have gone astray, each of us has turned to our own way... (Isaiah 53:6a)†

The question is: what will God do about our rebellion against him?

Step 1a

Without looking at page 46, fill in the blanks in the statements.

> We all reject _____ by running
>
> _____ our own way.
>
> By rebelling against _____, we damage
>
> _____, _____, and _____
>
> _____.

Check your answers, and make any corrections. Read the corrected version of the statements aloud, doing the drawing as you go.

Fill in the blanks in the Bible verse and transition statement.

> We all, like _____, have _____,
> each of us has _____...
> (Isaiah 53:____)
>
> **The _____ is: what will God _____**
> **our rebellion _____?**

Check your answers, and make any corrections. Read the corrected Bible verse and transition statement aloud.

If possible, wait some time (perhaps even 24 hours) before moving on to step 2.

Step 2

Fill in the blanks in the statements.

> We all _____
> by _____
> _____.
> By _____:
> we _____, _____, and
> _____.

Check your answers, and make any corrections. Read through the corrected version of the statements, doing the drawing as you go.

Without looking at page 48, fill in the blanks in the Bible verse and transition statement.

> We _____, _____, have _____
> _____, _____
> _____ own way... (Isaiah ____:____)
>
> **The _____: what will _____**
> **_____ our _____?**

Check your answers, and make any corrections. Read the corrected Bible verse and transition statement aloud.

If possible, wait some time (perhaps even 24 hours) before moving on to step 3.

Step 3

On a blank sheet of paper, write out the statements from memory, and then correct your version.

Read the corrected statements aloud while doing the drawing.

Repeat this process until you can say the statements perfectly while doing the drawing.

On a blank sheet of paper, write out the Bible verse and transition statement, and then make any corrections.

Read the corrected version aloud.

Repeat the process until you can say the Bible verse and transition statement perfectly.

3. Sin

Review

In pairs or triplets, take it in turns to see if you can repeat to each other from memory the two statements of point 2 of *Two Ways to Live*, and reproduce the drawing.

The story of sin

The common view among nearly all non-Christians (and even some Christians) is that sin is essentially rule-breaking. Most people think of sin in terms of individual acts of wrongdoing, such as stealing or murder or adultery. And that's how many of our dictionaries put it as well—for example, *Dictionary.com* defines sin as "transgression of divine law."

Under this definition, many people give themselves a pass. Although they admit that they do "transgress" from time to time, they also manage to keep some of the rules as well—they don't steal (or at least not often), and they manage not to commit adultery (at least most of the time), and they've never murdered anyone. What's more, they clearly don't "sin" nearly as much as a lot of *other* people, and they balance the ledger a bit by giving to charity or doing some voluntary work.

If sin is basically rule-breaking, I can see myself as a middling sort of performer. I may even have a decent chance of being acceptable to God.

But to define sin as "rule-breaking" is to define it in terms of its symptoms rather than the disease itself. And the disease, according to the Bible, is deep-rooted, chronic, and ultimately fatal. And it goes back to the very beginning of humanity's relationship with God.

Point 2 of *Two Ways to Live* summarizes the disease of sin like this:

We all reject God as our ruler by running our own lives our own way.

By rebelling against God's way, we damage ourselves, each other, and the world.

Once again, to begin to understand what these apparently simple statements contain, we need to go back to the beginning of the Bible.

> [1] Now the serpent was more crafty than any other beast of the field that the LORD God had made.
>
> He said to the woman, "Did God actually say, 'You shall not eat of any tree in the garden'?" [2] And the woman said to the serpent, "We may eat of the fruit of the trees in the garden, [3] but God said, 'You shall not eat of the fruit of the tree that is in the midst of the garden, neither shall you touch it, lest you die.'" [4] But the serpent said to the woman, "You will not surely die. [5] For God knows that when you eat of it your eyes will be opened, and you will be like God, knowing good and evil." [6] So when the woman saw that the tree was good for food, and that it was a delight to the eyes, and that the tree was to be desired to make one wise, she took of its fruit and ate, and she also gave some to her husband who was with her, and he ate. [7] Then the eyes of both were opened, and they knew that they were naked. And they sewed fig leaves together and made themselves loincloths. (Gen 3:1-7)

1. What arguments or other factors end up persuading Eve and Adam to eat from the tree?

2. What was their attitude towards God in doing this?

The early chapters of Genesis are foundational for our understanding of many key biblical ideas. That's certainly the case with what we read here about sin. Yet it's not the complete picture. As the Bible unfolds, we discover that the rebellious stance of Eve and Adam—taking matters into their own hands and deciding for themselves what would be for their good—is tragically played out in the heart of every human. Let's look at some biblical highlights (or lowlights).

In Psalm 51, David bemoans the sinful train wreck of his adultery with Bathsheba:

¹Have mercy on me, O God,
    according to your steadfast love;
according to your abundant mercy
    blot out my transgressions.
²Wash me thoroughly from my iniquity,
    and cleanse me from my sin!
³For I know my transgressions,
    and my sin is ever before me.
⁴Against you, you only, have I sinned
    and done what is evil in your sight,
so that you may be justified in your words
    and blameless in your judgment.
⁵Behold, I was brought forth in iniquity,
    and in sin did my mother conceive me.
        (Ps 51:1-5)

3. Notice all the different words or metaphors David uses to describe his actions and his character. What do you think this teaches us about the nature of sin?

4. Why do you think he says to God that "against you, *you only*, have I sinned"?

David speaks to God in some anguish as one of God's chosen people; in fact, as God's chosen king of Israel. But sin is by no means confined to Israel. In Romans 1-3, Paul argues that all of humanity shares the disease. Here's his classic description of how all the nations of the world react to God as creator:

> [18] For the wrath of God is revealed from heaven against all ungodliness and unrighteousness of men, who by their unrighteousness suppress the truth. [19] For what can be known about God is plain to them, because God has shown it to them. [20] For his invisible attributes, namely, his eternal power and divine nature, have been clearly perceived, ever since the creation of the world, in the things that have been made. So they are without excuse. [21] For although they knew God, they did not honor him as God or give thanks to him, but they

became futile in their thinking, and their foolish hearts were darkened. [22] Claiming to be wise, they became fools, [23] and exchanged the glory of the immortal God for images resembling mortal man and birds and animals and creeping things.

[24] Therefore God gave them up in the lusts of their hearts to impurity, to the dishonoring of their bodies among themselves, [25] because they exchanged the truth about God for a lie and worshiped and served the creature rather than the Creator, who is blessed forever! Amen. (Rom 1:18-25)

5. What can all people know about God, and how *should* they respond to that knowledge?

6. What do people do instead?

7. What are the consequences?

 The key concepts

*(Go to **matthiasmedia.com/learnthegospel** to watch bonus video 3a at this point, or read the following text aloud together.)*

a. Sin is a rejection of God

The essential nature of human sin—the underlying disease—is a *rejection of God as our ruler*. We rebel against his rightful claim over us as our creator, and try to step out from under his authority. As the drawing in point 2 of *Two Ways to Live* illustrates, we appoint ourselves king of our own lives.

This is why the little word "by" in the first statement is important. We reject God as our ruler not just by committing individual transgressions but *by* running our own lives our own way. We turn away from God, and declare ourselves to be in charge of our own selves and choices.

We see this in Genesis 3. It wasn't just that Eve and Adam disobeyed one particular command of God (not to eat of that particular tree). In doing so, they wanted to grasp knowledge and power that wasn't theirs. They wanted to take the place of God, and be like God themselves.

In a similar way, Romans 1 paints a picture of sin not just as individual acts of wrongdoing, but as an act of will that suppresses the truth about God and instead foolishly embraces the lie. The wickedness of humanity is that rather than worshipping and honoring and thanking our creator, we turn to worship and serve created things (see Romans 1:18-25).

This is the crucial first concept to understand about sin: that it is a willful, relational rejection of God as creator and ruler.

b. Universal and comprehensive

This rejection of God is a universal human phenomenon. We *all* reject God as our ruler. As the Bible verse for point 2 puts it: "We all, like sheep, have gone astray, each of us has turned to our own way..." (Isa 53:6a).[†]

This idea has particular relevance for religious people—whether churchgoers or people of other religions. We looked above at Romans 1, but in Romans 2 Paul turns the spotlight on his fellow Jews, and condemns them as also being under the power of sin. These were *very* religious people, but their diligent religious practice didn't fool God. He knew the state of their hearts—that they were every bit as rebellious against him as the most lawless, unchurched pagan.

We'll talk more about religious or moral people below, but at this point we should also note that the Bible teaches that sin is not only universal in its reach to every human, but *comprehensive* in its penetration of our whole personalities.

We see this in Romans 1:18-32. Humanity makes a willful and foolish choice to reject God; our *hearts* are darkened, and our *minds* become futile. Under the judgment of God, this in turn leads to our moral compass going completely astray, and we end up embracing and approving of all kinds of impure and unrighteous *actions*.

This is what is meant by the theological term "total depravity"—not that we are totally and utterly as evil as we can possibly be, but that every part of us is corrupted by sin: our minds, our will, our desires, our hearts, our actions, our total selves.

c. Consequences

There several consequences of our rebellion. One is that we become the objects of God's anger and judgment, but we'll come back to that in point 3 of *Two Ways to Live*.

The more immediate consequence is that by rebelling against God's way we "damage ourselves, each other, and the world" (as the outline puts it).

It starts with us damaging ourselves because, in rebelling against God and fleeing from his rule, we find ourselves not free and happy but enslaved to other rulers and forces. Ephesians 2 speaks of three influences or powers that we can't escape:

> And you were dead in the trespasses and sins in which you once walked, following the course of this world, following the prince of the power of the air, the spirit that is now at work in the sons of disobedience—among whom we all once lived in the passions of our flesh, carrying out the desires of the body and the mind, and were by nature children of wrath, like the rest of mankind. (Eph 2:1-3)

These are the triple powers of sin: a *sinful culture* all around us that pushes and pulls us in the wrong direction ("the course of this world"); *Satan* or the Evil One who is also at work in us because we have believed his lie that God is not God ("the prince of the power of the air"); and our own misdirected and distorted *passions and desires* ("the passions of our flesh").

And so we find ourselves trapped. We let ourselves and others down, and can't understand why. We rebel against God and set up our own little tinpot kingdom, only to discover that it is all going to hell.

At the intimate level, our marriages and friendships struggle and break apart. At a broader level, our society is marred by lying, cheating, killing, and all manner of injustice. In fact, we find ourselves alienated from the world as a whole, which now produces thorns and thistles for us, and groans with its own frustration and corruption (see Romans 8:20-22).

All these consequences flow from the one fateful act of will that we all share—the doomed choice to "reject God as our ruler by running our own lives our own way."

8. In your own life, when or where do you most often notice the impulse to "run your own life your own way"?

9. Think of the nicest person you know—whether a Christian or a non-Christian. Why do you find it hard to believe that they are a sinner?

 Alternatives

*(Go to **matthiasmedia.com/learnthegospel** to watch bonus video 3b at this point, or read the following text aloud together.)*

The biblical doctrine of sin is not only widely misunderstood; there are also three common alternative views of human nature.

a. We're all good

The first, which is very commonly believed and promoted in our secular humanist society, is that humanity is essentially good at heart. This flies in the face of history and experience, not to mention the nightly news. But many Western people believe it.

The most common form of this view is that factors outside us—such as the unjust structures of society or the dysfunctions of our upbringing—are really responsible for the wrong things we do. It's not me; it's the system. Society is to blame. It was lack of education. My parents messed me up.

But of course, society is made up of *people*; and if people are all basically good at heart, then where did the evil nature of society come from? Why is a group of people a corrupting influence when all the individuals in the group are supposed to be good at heart? Likewise, if it's really our parents' fault, why did they do that if they were really good people deep down?

Jesus pointed out the folly of this position when he said:

"What comes out of a person is what defiles him. For from within, out of the heart of man, come evil thoughts, sexual immorality, theft, murder, adultery, coveting, wickedness, deceit, sensuality, envy, slander, pride, foolishness. All these evil things come from within, and they defile a person." (Mark 7:20-23)

The humanist view tries to argue that we are made evil by forces outside of us. But Jesus points out the obvious truth: the problem lies within, not outside.

One particular form that the humanist view has taken at various points in history is that the external cause of our problems is not society as a whole, but *one group* within society that has seized power for itself and is now responsible for the corruption and injustice that we experience. *We* are good (that is, our particular tribe or group); the evil is the fault of the other group that has seized control and messed everything up. This "other" group may be defined economically, as it is in classical Marxism, or in terms of identity (such as race or gender), but the pattern is the same. My group and I are not evil; the problem is external to me. And if the "power group" can be overthrown, and all the victimized set free, then evil will be defeated, and goodness and harmony will flourish.

Again, this is demonstrably untrue in human history and experience. Whenever the old "power group" is overthrown, the new power group turns out to be just as corrupt. This is because, as Jesus taught us, the real problem is within each of our hearts.

b. Sincerity

The second alternative view is that there is no objective standard of wrongdoing or right-doing, and no God before whom we're accountable. Instead, the "goodness" of each person should be judged according to their *sincerity*—whether they have sincerely lived out their *own principles* with integrity and authenticity.

In this view, sin is breaking *your own* rules—the standards or principles you've adopted for yourself. And correspondingly, righteousness is sticking to your own principles with sincerity.

This view doesn't stand up to much scrutiny. Do we really want to say that Hitler or Stalin or Mao should be judged according to the sincerity with which they murderously followed their personal principles? If a psychopathic serial killer genuinely has no remorse or guilt about his actions, but sincerely believes they are legitimate, does that make them legitimate?

Sincerity is a good indication of... sincerity. But it can't be a measure of good and evil.

c. A spark of goodness

This is a Christian alternative view with a long history. It's the idea that although we do suffer from sin, and this makes us guilty before God, we're not *entirely* bad—there is a spark of goodness in us that waits to be fanned into flame. By various means, perhaps through church activities or religious practices, this seed of goodness within us can be nurtured and grown, and can lead to us becoming righteous people, acceptable to God.

The Bible is very clear. It is not that we are spiritually sick and in need of some therapy or medicine: we are *dead* in transgression and sin, and in need of new life breathed into us from outside. If sin is fundamentally rebellion against our creator, then that is what must be fixed—not just an incremental improvement in certain moral acts. If the relational rejection of God is not addressed and the relationship is not restored, then we are still stuck in sin, in rebellion, regardless of how many little old ladies we help across the street.

10. Which of these alternative views have you come across most often? If someone expressed this alternative view to you tomorrow, based on what you've learned, what would you say in response?

Summing up

The essence of the biblical doctrine of sin is the fracture in our relationship with God, initiated and sustained by us. We have rejected his rule over us and over our world as the creator—and this expresses itself in all manner of actions, thoughts, and attitudes that are contrary to God's will. Sin is a rebellion against the rightful claims of our creator over us.

This is why point 2 of *Two Ways to Live* requires point 1. Sin is a rebellion against the God who made us and rules us—not just against God in general, but against our maker, who has created us for his own purposes. Without God as creator and ruler, there is no sin.

The world doesn't understand this because it doesn't understand God as creator and ruler of all. And so it either denies the idea of sin altogether, or transforms it into "rule-breaking."

The other thing that our world finds curiously difficult to accept is that God will do anything about our rebellion against his rule. But an important aspect of the gospel is that God can do, has done, and will do something about our rejection of him.

And that leads us to the third point of *Two Ways to Live*, and to the reality of God's judgment.

Before next time

Reflect and pray about what you've learned in this chapter

Look back over this chapter. Make notes in the margin about truths that prompt you to give thanks and pray. Spend some time thanking God and asking him to write these truths in your heart.

If you watched the videos in your group, make sure you read those sections of text—and vice versa (if you read aloud the sections of text, watch the relevant videos).

Learn point 3 of *Two Ways to Live*: Judgment
Step 1

Read the statements aloud three times, tracing over the drawing as you do so.

God won't let us rebel against him forever. *(draw crown)*
God's punishment for rebellion is death and judgment. *(draw humanity)*

LEARN THE GOSPEL

Read the Bible verse and transition statement aloud three times.

> Just as people are destined to die once, and after that to face judgment... (Hebrews 9:27)[†]

> **This is hard to hear. It means that we are all in deep trouble. But it's not the end of the story.**

Step 1a
Without looking at page 68, fill in the blanks in the statements.

> God won't let us _____
>
> _____.
>
> God's _____ for rebellion is _____
>
> and _____.

Check your answers, and make any corrections. Read the corrected version of the statements aloud, doing the drawing as you go.

Fill in the blanks in the Bible verse and transition statement.

Just as people are destined to _____, and
after that to _____... (Hebrews 9:____)

**This is hard _____. It means that we are
all _____. But it's not
_____.**

Check your answers, and make any corrections. Read the
corrected Bible verse and transition statement aloud.

If possible, wait some time (perhaps even 24 hours)
before moving on to step 2.

Step 2
Fill in the blanks in the statements.

_____ rebel _____
_____.
_____ for _____
is _____ and _____.

Check your answers, and make any corrections. Read
the corrected version of the statements aloud, doing the
drawing as you go.

Without looking at page 70, fill in the blanks in the Bible verse and transition statement.

> _____
>
> die once, and _____
>
> judgment... (_____:___)
>
> **This is** _____**. It means** _____
>
> _____**. But** _____
>
> _____.

Check your answers, and make any corrections. Read the corrected Bible verse and transition statement aloud.

If possible, wait some time (perhaps even 24 hours) before moving on to step 3.

Step 3

On a blank sheet of paper, write out the statements from memory, and then correct your version.

Read the corrected statements aloud while doing the drawing.

Repeat this process until you can say the statements perfectly while doing the drawing.

On a blank sheet of paper, write out the Bible verse and transition statement, and then make any corrections.

Read the corrected version aloud.

Repeat the process until you can say the Bible verse and transition statement perfectly.

4. Judgment

Review

In pairs or triplets, take it in turns to see if you can repeat to each other from memory the two statements of point 3 of *Two Ways to Live*, and reproduce the drawing.

The God who judges

As soon as we begin to speak of God's judgment, we speak about something that the world regards as unpopular and distasteful.

This is no reason not to talk about it. But it gives us every reason to be very clear in our understanding of God's judgment. In fact, it is essential that we understand judgment, because without it (as we shall see), the death of Jesus makes very little sense.

Point 3 of *Two Ways to Live* summarizes the judgment of God against our sin like this:

> God won't let us rebel against him forever.
> God's punishment for rebellion is death and judgment.

Throughout the Bible, God is presented as a holy, righteous, infinitely good God, who judges every person according to what they have done.

When Moses is laying down the law for the Israelites before they enter the promised land, for example, he makes it very clear what God will do to them if they disobey him:

> [16] "You know how we lived in the land of Egypt, and how we came through the midst of the nations through which you passed. [17] And you have seen their detestable things, their idols of wood and

stone, of silver and gold, which were among them. ¹⁸ Beware lest there be among you a man or woman or clan or tribe whose heart is turning away today from the LORD our God to go and serve the gods of those nations. Beware lest there be among you a root bearing poisonous and bitter fruit, ¹⁹ one who, when he hears the words of this sworn covenant, blesses himself in his heart, saying, 'I shall be safe, though I walk in the stubbornness of my heart.' This will lead to the sweeping away of moist and dry alike. ²⁰ The LORD will not be willing to forgive him, but rather the anger of the LORD and his jealousy will smoke against that man, and the curses written in this book will settle upon him, and the LORD will blot out his name from under heaven. ²¹ And the LORD will single him out from all the tribes of Israel for calamity, in accordance with all the curses of the covenant written in this Book of the Law." (Deut 29:16-21)

1. What attitudes or behavior did the people need to avoid?

2. What words or phrases describe God's response to those who did such things? What does this tell us about God's character?

3. How do you think it could be right for God to be "jealous"?

Some people think that God's judgment is mainly an Old Testament thing. In the New Testament (they believe), the fiery God of the Old Testament has calmed down a bit, and become more loving.

But this misunderstands both testaments. As an example, take a look at this passage from Paul's second letter to the Thessalonians:

⁵This is evidence of the righteous judgment of God, that you may be considered worthy of the kingdom of God, for which you are also suffering—⁶since indeed God considers it just to repay with affliction those who afflict you, ⁷and to grant relief to you who are afflicted as well as to us, when the Lord Jesus is revealed from heaven with his mighty angels ⁸in flaming fire, inflicting vengeance on those who do not know God and on those who do not obey the gospel of our Lord Jesus. ⁹They will suffer the punishment of eternal destruction, away from the presence of the Lord and from the glory of his might, ¹⁰when he comes on that day to be glorified in his saints, and to be marveled at among all who have believed, because our testimony to you was believed. (2 Thess 1:5-10)

4. What similarities and differences do you see between this passage and the passage we looked at above (Deuteronomy 29)?

5. When and how will the judgment come? And by whom?

6. What will the punishment be?

▶ The key concepts

*(Go to **matthiasmedia.com/learnthegospel** to watch bonus video 4a at this point, or read the following text aloud together.)*

Whenever we make anything for any purpose, we assess (or "judge") whether that thing has achieved its purpose. Was the cake a success?

We've already looked at *God's purposes* for creating the world and humanity (in chapter 2). God created humanity to live as the rulers of his world under his authority; to live according to his ways and his will, and to extend and represent his rule in the creation. Our rejection of God's rule—our rebellion against his purposes for us—leads to a negative judgment against us. Any good, faithful, righteous creator would respond this way.

God certainly does, and this is seen throughout the Bible. In Proverbs, for example, there is a long list of those whom God assures us will "not go unpunished": anyone who has sex with his neighbor's wife; anyone who is arrogant in heart, or is a false witness, or who hastens to be rich; anyone who "mocks the poor," because in so doing he insults his maker (Prov 6:29, 16:5, 19:5, 28:20, 17:5). All these behaviors violate the purposes God has for his creation and are therefore judged negatively by him.

The Scriptures constantly assure us that the righteous response of God to our rebellion, and to all the sinful behaviors that stem from it, is judgment and punishment.

God's judgment is delivered in three main ways.

a. First way: God punishes now in history

The Bible says that God punishes and judges humanity now, in our present human experience.

This begins with the punishment of Adam and Eve. We all now live outside the garden in a world under God's judgment—a world of pain in childbirth, of thorns and thistles, and of inevitable death. Our world is subjected to futility, as it says in Romans 8:20-25. The whole creation is in bondage to decay, awaiting liberation. Whenever we experience sickness, pain, or decay, we are witnessing God's judgment against our rebellious world—although any particular sickness or suffering is not necessarily a particular judgment against a person's sin (see John 9:1-3).

God's present judgment against us and our world is sometimes delivered through human agents. The pagan King Cyrus (in Isaiah 45) is God's anointed instrument of judgment against Israel. The government (in Romans 13:1-7) wields the sword on God's behalf to punish wrongdoers.

God's judgment can also be seen in his giving sinful people up to the foolish and destructive consequences of their rebellion, as Romans 1:18-32 so powerfully describes. God's judgment is being revealed now against the godlessness and unrighteousness of humanity. (We have already seen this in point 2 in the way our rebellion damages "ourselves, each other, and the world.")

b. Second way: God punishes by mortality

Perhaps the most striking way God's judgment is revealed in history is through *death*. We all die, not because it is "natural" but because we are under the judgment of God. God's warning to Adam and Eve was that if they ate of the tree of the knowledge of good and evil, against his command, then "in the day that you eat of it you shall surely die" (Gen 2:17).

And this is precisely what happens. They go ahead and eat of it, and God's judgment is to drive them from his presence and declare that they will return to the dust from which they were made (Gen 3:19). The New Testament picks up this idea: sin and death came into the world through Adam, says Paul, and spread to all of us because all of us sinned (Rom 5:12). The wages of sin is death (Rom 6:23).

This is very important for understanding why Jesus had to die, and what his death meant—but more of that in our next chapter.

c. Third way: God punishes at the end of the world

Even though death is the punishment for sin, the Bible also says that there is an existence beyond death, and that judgment also takes place in that realm. As the Bible verse for point 3 says: "Just as people are destined to die once, and after that to face judgment..." (Heb 9:27).[†]

God's judgment will also be revealed to us on what Romans 2:5 calls "the day of wrath." Acts 17:31 says that God has fixed a day on which he will judge the world in righteousness by a man whom he has appointed—the resurrected man, Jesus Christ.

This idea is taught throughout the Bible: a day is coming when not just individuals but the whole created order will suffer God's anger and judgment; a day of reckoning and destruction, when the heavens will pass away with a roar and the heavenly bodies will be dissolved, and the earth and the works that are done on it will be exposed (2 Pet 3:10).

On that day, those who have continued in rebellion against God will suffer what at various points in Scripture is called "hell" or "eternal destruction." Second Thessalonians describes this final judgment very starkly:

> ...when the Lord Jesus is revealed from heaven with his mighty angels in flaming fire, inflicting vengeance on those who do not know God and on those who do not obey the gospel of our Lord Jesus. They will suffer the punishment of eternal destruction, away from the presence of the Lord and from the glory of his might... (2 Thess 1:7-9)

This is another way of describing hell. It is not annihilation, but eternal ruin—like the smoking rubble of a once-great house.

We might ask then: If this punishment is just and righteous and is due to humanity, why has it not yet come?

Second Peter 3 teaches us that God is delaying the final judgment of the world because of his kindness and patience, to give people time to repent. Then, as now, sinful people presume on this patience of God and scoff. They say that judgment hasn't come because it will never come.

The mocking rejection of the idea of God's judgment is not new. It happened in the Garden of Eden (Gen 3:4); it was happening when 2 Peter was written; and it still happens today. In our world, it takes the form of various objections or alternatives to the idea of judgment, which we will look at below.

7. Where do you see God's judgment in the world now? How have you experienced God's judgment in your life?

8. How do you feel about the different aspects of God's judgment? Does any of what we've looked at bother you or raise questions for you?

▶ Alternatives

*(Go to **matthiasmedia.com/learnthegospel** to watch bonus video 4b at this point, or read the following text aloud together.)*

a. No punishment, because God is love

It is very common for people to object to the idea of judgment on the grounds that God is love, and is not the kind of God who would judge anyone or send them to hell. It is inconsistent and impossible, they argue, for God to be infinitely loving and also a righteous judge who is angry at sin.

But this misunderstands both love and judgment. Judgment is not the opposite of love; *indifference* is the opposite of love. When you don't care about what is right, or aren't prepared to do anything about injustice—when you sit back and let evil triumph—how does that express love? Love cares enough about goodness and about people to become righteously angry and indignant at evil and injustice, and to want to see justice done. Loving parents care enough about their children to discipline and punish them for their good. Indifferent, negligent parents, who let their children run wild, are showing them no love.

Love without justice and judgment is ultimately just sentimentality. In fact, if there is no judgment, there is no justice and no accountability. Without the concept of judgment, nothing we do really matters.

All the same, we shouldn't misrepresent the judgment of God as if it is just like the anger and judgment of a human parent. Unlike us, God is slow to anger, and his anger is never hasty or spiteful or self-centered. It's not as if God loses his temper. And unlike our anger, God's anger is always righteous; it is always perfectly appropriate as a response to evil.

b. Impersonal consequences

There is a particular Christian alternative view that emphasizes the love of God in the gospel, and either diminishes or entirely rejects the idea that God is a righteous judge. In this way of thinking, sin is seen as an impersonal breaking of rules which leads to certain bad consequences, including erecting a barrier between us and God. In this view, sin is not a *personal* rebellion against God, but an impersonal rejection of certain rules and standards. And so in this view, God is not *personally* angry at us, nor does he judge or punish us personally for our sin. The bad things that happen as a result of our sin are just the sad but inevitable consequences of our actions.

Ironically, by downplaying the reality of God's personal anger and judgment against us and our sin, this view actually makes it much harder to grasp how deep the love of God is in sending his Son to take the punishment for our sin. By trying to have love without judgment, this view makes the cross incomprehensible and empties God's love of its power.

c. Universalism

The third common alternative is that everyone everywhere will be saved. "Universalism" (as it is often called) teaches that there are many roads and many paths, but they are all leading to the same destination. And God will make sure that everyone gets there. In the end, no one will be judged and punished.

The trouble with universalism, as with nearly all heresies, is that it is half true. It is a godly instinct to want everyone to be saved (for God has no pleasure in the death of a sinner). But the Bible is quite clear that not everyone will be saved.

In some ways, the problem with universalism (and with most alternatives to the concept of God's judgment) is a lack of awareness or understanding of why judgment is necessary. In other words, it's a misunderstanding or denial of the nature of human sin and rebellion (point 2 of *Two Ways to Live*). It doesn't see all humanity as being hopelessly trapped in rebellion against their creator and as needing salvation from outside, but instead sees humanity as being on a quest to find God by various means.

But if the Bible's diagnosis of our disease is true—that we are all rebels against God—then its prognosis of the outcome is equally true: that if we continue in rebellion, we will receive the judgment that rebels deserve.

9. How are God's anger and judgment different from ours?

10. If you were going to explain in your own words how God's judgment relates to his love, what would you say?

Summing up

It's very important to understand the judgment of God, and to be able to explain it clearly and without embarrassment. God's judgment doesn't come out of the blue; it's not arbitrary or cruel. It is the necessary implication of two prior truths: firstly, that God is the ruler of the world because he made the world; and secondly, that we have all rebelled against our good creator and ruler.

Without judgment—without the reality of our responsibility and accountability before our creator—our actions are ultimately without moral meaning. They are neither good nor bad.

And of course, without the reality of judgment as God's response to our rebellion, God's *other* response—

of mercy through the death of his Son—makes very little sense. Where there is no judgment, there can be no mercy, for there is nothing to be forgiven.

Before next time

Reflect and pray about what you've learned in this chapter

Look back over this chapter. Make notes in the margin about truths that prompt you to give thanks and pray. Spend some time thanking God and asking him to write these truths in your heart.

If you watched the videos in your group, make sure you read those sections of text—and vice versa (if you read aloud the sections of text, watch the relevant videos).

Learn point 4 of *Two Ways to Live*: Jesus' death

Step 1

Read the statements aloud three times, tracing over the drawing as you do so.

Because of his love, God sent his Son into the world: the man Jesus Christ. *(draw world, Jesus' body without arms, and J)* Jesus always lived under God's rule. *(draw crown)*
But Jesus took our punishment by dying in our place.
(draw Jesus' arms horizontally to indicate death on cross)

Read the Bible verse and transition statement aloud three times.

> We all, like sheep, have gone astray, each of us has turned to our own way; and the LORD has laid on him the iniquity of us all. (Isaiah 53:6)†
>
> **But that's not all.**

Step 1a

Without looking at page 88, fill in the blanks in the statements.

> Because of _____, God sent _____
> _____: _____ Jesus Christ.
> Jesus always lived _____.
> But Jesus took _____ by
> _____ place.

Check your answers, and make any corrections. Read the corrected version of the statements aloud, doing the drawing as you go.

Fill in the blanks in the Bible verse and transition statement.

> We all, like _____, have _____,
> each of us has _____;
> and the LORD _____ the
> _____ of us all. (Isaiah 53:___)
>
> **But** _____.

Check your answers, and make any corrections. Read the corrected Bible verse and transition statement aloud.

If possible, wait some time (perhaps even 24 hours) before moving on to step 2.

Step 2

Fill in the blanks in the statements.

> _____ love, _____
> into the world: _____.
> _____God's rule.
> _____ punishment
> _____ in _____.

Check your answers, and make any corrections. Read the corrected version of the statements aloud, doing the drawing as you go.

Without looking at page 90, fill in the blanks in the Bible verse and transition statement.

We _____, _____, _____ gone
_____, _____ turned
_____; _____
laid on _____ iniquity _____.
(_____:___)

_____ all.

Check your answers, and make any corrections. Read the corrected Bible verse and transition statement aloud.

If possible, wait some time (perhaps even 24 hours) before moving on to step 3.

Step 3

On a blank sheet of paper, write out the statements from memory, and then correct your version.

Read the corrected statements aloud while doing the drawing.

Repeat this process until you can say the statements perfectly while doing the drawing.

On a blank sheet of paper, write out the Bible verse and transition statement, and then make any corrections.

Read the corrected version aloud.

Repeat the process until you can say the Bible verse and transition statement perfectly.

5. Jesus' death

Review

In pairs or triplets, take it in turns to see if you can repeat to each other from memory the first *four* points of *Two Ways to Live*, and reproduce the drawings.

The crux of the gospel

We're getting now to the center of the gospel pronouncement itself—that the crucified and risen Jesus is God's king who offers salvation and forgiveness to all. Point 5 draws that together and proclaims it.

However, there is no way to point 5 except through point 4—no path to the resurrection and lordship of Jesus as king and savior except via the cross. The cross was the event that so scandalized Jesus' contemporaries, and it still confounds and offends people today. None of the Jewish leaders of his day, or even his own disciples, expected God's glorious king to die a humiliating death on a Roman cross. And yet Jesus knew that this was the plan of God—that only by taking the punishment for our sins on the cross could he rise as the conquering king to offer forgiveness to all.

If we're going to learn the gospel, we need to understand the crucifixion of Jesus.

Point 4 of *Two Ways to Live* summarizes the meaning of Jesus' death like this:

> Because of his love, God sent his Son into the world: the man Jesus Christ. Jesus always lived under God's rule. But Jesus took our punishment by dying in our place.

Let's start by looking at one of the most significant Old Testament passages about Jesus' death—the famous prophecy of Isaiah 52-53. This passage speaks about a "servant" of God who will be "exalted" and yet whose appearance will be marred and shocking (Isa 52:13-14). As you read what the prophecy says about the servant, underline each phrase that describes him doing something on behalf of others.

³ He was despised and rejected by men,
>   a man of sorrows and acquainted with grief;
> and as one from whom men hide their faces
>   he was despised, and we esteemed him not.

⁴ Surely he has borne our griefs
>   and carried our sorrows;
> yet we esteemed him stricken,
>   smitten by God, and afflicted.
> ⁵ But he was pierced for our transgressions;
>   he was crushed for our iniquities;
> upon him was the chastisement that brought us
>   peace,
>   and with his wounds we are healed.
> ⁶ All we like sheep have gone astray;
>   we have turned—every one—to his own way;
> and the LORD has laid on him
>   the iniquity of us all.

⁷ He was oppressed, and he was afflicted,
>   yet he opened not his mouth;
> like a lamb that is led to the slaughter,

and like a sheep that before its shearers is silent,
    so he opened not his mouth.
[8] By oppression and judgment he was taken away;
    and as for his generation, who considered
that he was cut off out of the land of the living,
    stricken for the transgression of my people?
[9] And they made his grave with the wicked
    and with a rich man in his death,
although he had done no violence,
    and there was no deceit in his mouth.

[10] Yet it was the will of the LORD to crush him;
    he has put him to grief;
when his soul makes an offering for guilt,
    he shall see his offspring; he shall prolong his
        days;
the will of the LORD shall prosper in his hand.
[11] Out of the anguish of his soul he shall see and be
        satisfied;
by his knowledge shall the righteous one, my
        servant,
    make many to be accounted righteous,
    and he shall bear their iniquities.
[12] Therefore I will divide him a portion with the
        many,
    and he shall divide the spoil with the strong,
because he poured out his soul to death
    and was numbered with the transgressors;

yet he bore the sin of many,
    and makes intercession for the transgressors.
        (Isa 53:3-12)

1. What did you notice that the "servant" does or has done to him for the sake of others?

2. What is God's (or the LORD's) role in this? What actions does God take?

3. What *consequences* or *outcomes* flow from the actions of the servant:

- for others?

- for the servant?

Turning to the New Testament, let's dig into a Bible passage that teaches us about the cross from multiple angles. As you read these extraordinary words from 2 Corinthians 5, underline or mark any phrases or sentences that explain what Christ's death was about—what it meant or achieved.

> [14] For the love of Christ controls us, because we have concluded this: that one has died for all, therefore all have died; [15] and he died for all, that those who live might no longer live for themselves but for him who for their sake died and was raised.
>
> [16] From now on, therefore, we regard no one according to the flesh. Even though we once regarded Christ according to the flesh, we regard him thus no longer. [17] Therefore, if anyone is in Christ, he is a new creation. The old has passed away; behold, the new has come. [18] All this is from God, who through Christ reconciled us to himself and gave us the ministry of reconciliation; [19] that is, in Christ God was reconciling the world to himself, not counting their trespasses against them, and entrusting to us the message of reconciliation. [20] Therefore, we are ambassadors for Christ, God making his appeal through us. We implore you on behalf of Christ, be reconciled to God. [21] For our sake he made him to be sin who knew no sin, so that in him we might become the righteousness of God. (2 Cor 5:14-21)

There are three remarkable descriptions in this passage of what Jesus' death was about. Let's look at each one more closely.

4. Read verses 14-17 again carefully. What was happening when Christ died? What do you think this means?

5. What was the purpose or outcome of this? (See especially verses 15 and 17.)

6. Now look more closely at verses 18-19. How do these verses describe what God achieved through Christ's death and how he achieved it?

7. The third description of Christ's death is in verse 21. How is it similar to or different from the other descriptions? What do you think it adds?

The key concepts

*(Go to **matthiasmedia.com/learnthegospel** to watch bonus video 5 at this point, or read the following text aloud together.)*

There are three figures in the two profound passages we've just looked at—God, Jesus (the servant, the Christ), and humanity.

Jesus stands in the middle. He is related to God and to humanity, and his death reconciles God and humanity. To understand how this can be, let's look at each of those two key relationships—between Jesus and God, and between Jesus and humanity.

a. Jesus and God

There is only one God, but within the unity of God there are three persons—Father, Son, and Spirit. We cannot understand or explain the death of Jesus without affirming that *Jesus is God's own Son*; that Jesus himself is God, and one with his Father.

Why is Jesus' divinity essential to the cross?

If Jesus was only a man—even the best of men—his sacrifice could, at the very most, have redeemed the life of one other sinful person (and Psalm 49:7-9 casts doubt even on that).

However, the Bible says that Jesus' death was of sufficient value to deal with the sins of the whole world (1 John 2:2). This is because of the infinite value of Jesus' own divine person. God himself was on the cross, in the person of his Son, bearing the penalty and judgment not for his own sin, but for that of countless others.

Just as importantly, because the Son is one with the Father, the sacrifice of Jesus was not unjust. Some people have raised this objection to the substitutionary death of Jesus. They regard it as immoral that God should punish an innocent third party (like Jesus) for the sins of other people. How can that meet the perfect standards of justice of the holy God? And it seems like a fair point: If I commit a sin, how can it be fair for some other person to step in and be punished for it?

But because Jesus is one with his Father, *there is no third party*. On the cross, God was taking the punishment for our sins upon himself. He was not deflecting it onto some innocent bystander, but absorbing and paying the full cost himself.

To reflect this, the *Two Ways to Live* outline identifies Jesus as God's Son: "Because of his love, God sent *his Son* into the world."

But the outline then goes on to identify the Son as "the man Jesus Christ."

b. Jesus and humanity

It is equally important to understand Jesus' humanity. It is essential that in sending his own divine Son into the world, God sent him as fully man—because if Jesus was not man, he could not act as a representative or substitute for humans.

Jesus was a flesh-and-blood man. He was "made like his brothers in every respect, so that he might become a merciful and faithful high priest in the service of God, to make propitiation for the sins of the people" (Heb 2:17).

We will look at what "propitiation" means shortly, but at this point we need to notice that Jesus was a human, like us, so that he could represent us before God.

Of course, Jesus was like us in every way except one: he was without sin. Jesus "always lived under God's rule." This echoes point 1 of *Two Ways to Live*: humanity was created to rule the world under God, and to live under his rule. Unlike anyone before or since, Jesus did this. He did not reject God, or rebel against his ways. He did no damage to himself or others or the world, and he deserved no judgment or punishment, in this life or the next.

He came, in other words, as the perfect man, the one who finally did what God had created man to do: to rule the word under his authority. We will see (in the next chapter) that this is indeed what the risen Lord Jesus now does.

But Jesus was punished. He died.

c. The heart of the cross

The New Testament describes the effects of Jesus' death in a number of ways—it achieved reconciliation between man and God; it enabled God to declare previously unrighteous people now righteous or "justified"; it redeemed us from slavery; it defeated the power of Satan; and so on.

At the heart of all these different descriptions is the essential thing that Jesus did on the cross: he *propitiated* God as our *substitute*.

What does this mean?

We know what a "substitute" is. It's someone who takes the place of someone else, who acts on behalf of, or instead of, someone else. On the cross, Jesus was stepping in to act for us, instead of us, in our place (see Rom 5:8; Gal 3:13). And we saw above that Jesus could do this because he truly was a man who shared our flesh and blood.

What did he do as our substitute? He "propitiated" God.

To "propitiate" someone means to turn aside their anger or hostility. The Old Testament sacrificial system was built on this idea. The blood of sacrificed animals was accepted by God as a means of *turning aside his anger* at the sin of Israel.

This is what Jesus does on the cross. As both Son of God and perfect man, he steps in as our substitute and turns the righteous anger and judgment of God *away from us and onto himself*. The punishment from God that was due to us falls upon him instead.

This is why point 3 of *Two Ways to Live* is so essential for understanding point 4. Without understanding that we all deserve death and judgment as God's punishment for our rebellion, we cannot make sense of why *the substitutionary death of Jesus* saves us.

But it did save us, because Jesus died the death that we all deserved to die.

8. Discuss together: Have you learned something new about the cross so far in this chapter? Or had something clarified?

9. What do you think is the most difficult thing about the cross for people to accept?

A common alternative

The most common alternative to seeing Jesus' substitutionary death as a propitiation to turn aside God's anger and judgment is to regard it merely as the ultimate example of love and self-sacrifice.

This view of Jesus' death is usually coupled with a lack of belief in the idea of judgment. If you don't believe that God will judge our sin, then why was Jesus' death necessary, let alone important? If there is no punishment of death for sin, and therefore no need for a substitutionary death for sinners, then why would God send his Son to die?

Well, it is argued, it was to provide a supreme example of love so that we might follow in Jesus' footsteps and love other people, and so be acceptable to God. There is a half-truth in this, of course—Jesus' death was indeed the ultimate example of love, and we should imitate his self-sacrificial humility (see, for example, Philippians 2:1-11).

But this explanation doesn't help—because Jesus' death could only have been a supreme act of love if it achieved something on behalf of others (i.e. if it was an act of bearing someone else's punishment so that they could be forgiven). If it was not, then it is hard to see how simply dying functions an act of love. It's like saying to your wife and children: "I'm going to show how much I love you by flinging myself off this cliff." What does such an act achieve, brave though it might be? What does it do for your wife and children, except leave them to grieve a lost husband and father?

Jesus' death truly was an act of love—but it only makes sense as "love" if it achieved something. And the New Testament is very clear on what it does achieve: it turns aside the righteous and just judgment of God upon humanity because of our rebellion against him, and thus makes possible forgiveness and reconciliation between God and man.

Summing up

There are obvious connections between what we have been saying about the death of Jesus and the material in the first three points of *Two Ways to Live*. In fact, we can perhaps see why points 1-3 are so important in order for us to understand point 4: they help us grasp the depth of God's love at the cross.

Since we are God's good creation, and owe him all honor and glory and obedience as our maker, then our rebellion against him makes us guilty and worthy of his judgment. And that judgment is death.

Yet in his extraordinary kindness and grace, God sent his own Son to suffer that judgment, to take our punishment by dying in our place.

Before next time

Reflect and pray about what you've learned in this chapter

Look back over this chapter. Make notes in the margin about truths that prompt you to give thanks and pray. Spend some time thanking God and asking him to write these truths in your heart.

If you watched the video in your group, make sure you read that section of text—and vice versa (if you read aloud the section of text, watch the relevant video).

Learn point 5 of *Two Ways to Live*: Jesus' resurrection

Step 1

Read the statements aloud three times, tracing over the drawing as you do so.

> God raised Jesus to life again as the ruler and judge of the world. *(draw world and crown)* Jesus has conquered death, now brings forgiveness and new life, and will return in glory. *(draw J inside crown)*

Read the Bible verse and transition statement aloud three times.

> Praise be to the God and Father of our Lord Jesus Christ! In his great mercy he has given us new birth into a living hope through the resurrection of Jesus Christ from the dead... (1 Peter 1:3)†
>
> **Well, where does that leave us? It leaves us with a clear choice between two ways to live.**

Step 1a

Without looking up, fill in the blanks in the statements.

> God raised _____ as
>
> _____ and _____ of the world.
>
> Jesus has _____ , now brings
>
> _____ and _____ , and will
>
> _____ .

LEARN THE GOSPEL

Check your answers, and make any corrections. Read the corrected version of the statements aloud, doing the drawing as you go.

Without looking at page 108, fill in the blanks in the Bible verse and transition statement.

Praise be to _____ of our

_____! In _____

_____ he has given us _____ into a

_____ through the _____

_____ the dead...

(1 Peter 1:___)

Well, where does that _____? It
leaves us with _____ between _____

_____.

Check your answers, and make any corrections. Read the corrected Bible verse and transition statement aloud.

If possible, wait some time (perhaps even 24 hours) before moving on to step 2.

Step 2

Fill in the blanks in the statements.

God _____ again

_____ judge _____

_____ .

_____ death, _____

_____ and new life, and

_____ glory.

Check your answers, and make any corrections. Read the corrected version of the statements aloud, doing the drawing as you go.

Fill in the blanks in the Bible verse and transition statement.

_____ God and Father

_____ Christ! _____

_____ mercy he has _____

_____ a living hope _____

_____

the dead... (1 Peter ___:___)

Well, _____ **us? It**

_____ **a** _____

_____ **live.**

Check your answers, and make any corrections. Read the corrected Bible verse and transition statement aloud.

If possible, wait some time (perhaps even 24 hours) before moving on to step 3.

Step 3

On a blank sheet of paper, write out the statements from memory, and then correct your version.

Read the corrected statements aloud while doing the drawing.

Repeat this process until you can say the statements perfectly while doing the drawing.

On a blank sheet of paper, write out the Bible verse and transition statement, and then make any corrections.

Read the corrected version aloud.

Repeat the process until you can say the Bible verse and transition statement perfectly.

6. Jesus' resurrection

Review

In pairs or triplets, take it in turns to see if you can repeat to each other from memory *points 4 and 5* of *Two Ways to Live*, and reproduce the drawings.

The essential resurrection

If there is one aspect of the gospel (and of *Two Ways to Live*) that Christians frequently fail to understand, it is the resurrection of Jesus Christ from the dead. Judging by many modern presentations of the gospel, we often don't feel that very much is lost if we skip past the subject of the resurrection quite quickly.

Not so in the New Testament. As we've already briefly seen (in chapter 1), the proclamation of Jesus as the resurrected lord and king is at the heart of the gospel "newsflash." In fact, in the evangelistic sermons of Acts the resurrection is spoken about *more* than the death of Jesus—which is amazing to us, and should alert us to a potential problem with our gospel understanding.

Point 5 of *Two Ways to Live* summarizes the vital message of the resurrection like this:

> God raised Jesus to life again as the ruler and judge of the world.
> Jesus has conquered death, now brings forgiveness and new life, and will return in glory.

The first thing to realize is that in the Bible "the resurrection" is a broader and bigger topic in its own right, which we need to know something about if we are going to make sense of the resurrection of Jesus.

In the Bible generally, "the resurrection" is a way of

talking about *the judgment day* at the end of the world when the kingdom of God is finally established. It's the time that Jesus speaks about in John 5:28-29 when "all who are in the tombs will hear his voice and come out, those who have done good to the resurrection of life, and those who have done evil to the resurrection of judgment."

In much the same way, when Jesus is talking to Martha about her dead brother Lazarus, he says to her, "Your brother will rise again." And Martha answers, "I know that he will rise again in the resurrection on the last day" (John 11:23-24).

Martha knows that the resurrection is something that will happen to everyone on the last day (including Lazarus). But then Jesus says to Martha: *"I am the resurrection and the life"* (John 11:25).

In a way that Martha doesn't understand (and perhaps most of us don't), Jesus is claiming that the "resurrection"—the judgment day when the kingdom of God will be established—has already arrived in his own person. We will come back to what this means.

But with that background in mind, let's turn to one of the most important passages in the New Testament about the resurrection of Jesus: Peter's speech at Pentecost in Acts 2. We normally think of this as a passage all about the pouring out of the Spirit. But as we look at the climax of the sermon, we find that the real point is not so much the Spirit, but the One who has poured out this Spirit:

[22] "Men of Israel, hear these words: Jesus of Nazareth, a man attested to you by God with mighty works and wonders and signs that God did through him in your midst, as you yourselves know— [23] this Jesus, delivered up according to the definite plan and foreknowledge of God, you crucified and killed by the hands of lawless men. [24] God raised him up, loosing the pangs of death, because it was not possible for him to be held by it. [25] For David says concerning him,

> "'I saw the Lord always before me,
>> for he is at my right hand that I may not be shaken;
> [26] therefore my heart was glad, and my tongue rejoiced;
>> my flesh also will dwell in hope.
> [27] For you will not abandon my soul to Hades,
>> or let your Holy One see corruption.
> [28] You have made known to me the paths of life;
>> you will make me full of gladness with your presence.'

[29] "Brothers, I may say to you with confidence about the patriarch David that he both died and was buried, and his tomb is with us to this day. [30] Being therefore a prophet, and knowing that God had sworn with an oath to him that he would set one of his descendants on his throne,

[31] he foresaw and spoke about the resurrection of the Christ, that he was not abandoned to Hades, nor did his flesh see corruption. [32] This Jesus God raised up, and of that we all are witnesses. [33] Being therefore exalted at the right hand of God, and having received from the Father the promise of the Holy Spirit, he has poured out this that you yourselves are seeing and hearing. [34] For David did not ascend into the heavens, but he himself says,

> "'The Lord said to my Lord,
> "Sit at my right hand,
>> [35] until I make your enemies your footstool."'

[36] Let all the house of Israel therefore know for certain that God has made him both Lord and Christ, this Jesus whom you crucified."

[37] Now when they heard this they were cut to the heart, and said to Peter and the rest of the apostles, "Brothers, what shall we do?" [38] And Peter said to them, "Repent and be baptized every one of you in the name of Jesus Christ for the forgiveness of your sins, and you will receive the gift of the Holy Spirit." (Acts 2:22-38)

1. Having been raised by God from death, what position does Jesus now occupy?

2. How does this relate to the promises of the Old Testament?

3. According to this passage, what does Jesus do as "Lord and Christ"?

4. As he finishes his talk, what does Peter:

   - call on his hearers to do?

- promise them that God will do?

5. Peter doesn't go into detail in this passage about how "the forgiveness of your sins" is now available through the risen Jesus Christ. How would you explain to a friend why the resurrected Jesus is able to offer forgiveness of sins?

From Peter's famous sermon to the gathered crowd of Jewish listeners in Acts 2, let's turn to another very famous sermon in the book of Acts—Paul's address to the pagan Athenians in Acts 17. In the first half of his speech, Paul establishes for his listeners that God is the creator and sustainer of the whole world (rather like *Two Ways to Live* does!), and that the human impulse to worship idols rather than the true God is pretty stupid. Then he comes to the climax of his sermon:

[30] "The times of ignorance God overlooked, but now he commands all people everywhere to repent, [31] because he has fixed a day on which he will judge the world in righteousness by a man whom he has appointed; and of this he has given assurance to all by raising him from the dead."

[32] Now when they heard of the resurrection of the dead, some mocked. But others said, "We will hear you again about this." (Acts 17:30-32)

6. What does the resurrection of Jesus prove or demonstrate?

7. Who is this relevant for?

8. What response does this news require from its hearers?

9. The resurrected Jesus Christ is a man: true or false? Why does this matter?

▶ The key concepts

*(Go to **matthiasmedia.com/learnthegospel** to watch bonus video 6a at this point, or read the following text aloud together.)*

Have you begun to see why the resurrection of Jesus is so central to the gospel? It's all connected with judgment, which (remember) is what "resurrection" is about.

The resurrection means *first* of all that Jesus is *now the ruler and judge of the world.*

This is what the title "Christ" means—the promised king who would sit on the throne of David and rule over all the world for all time (2 Sam 7:12-16). Being ruler or king of all means that Jesus is the *judge of all.*

We're perhaps not used to thinking of kings as being judges, but it was a common idea in the ancient world. The king was supposed to bring justice—to right wrongs and to punish the wicked. This is the position God has appointed the risen Jesus to occupy. He is the one who will return in glory on the day that God has appointed, to rule and judge the whole world.

The "newsflash" of the gospel, then, is that God's long-promised king has risen to his throne as the lord and judge of all. The judgment day has been set, when all the evils and injustices of the world will be put right. And the man who has been appointed as the judge on that day is the risen Jesus Christ.

This is also good news in a *second* way, because the risen Jesus is the same Jesus who died to *save us from God's judgment*. In fact, as we said in the previous chapter, at the cross Jesus took the judgment of God for our sins upon himself. The resurrection shows that Jesus' sacrifice of "propitiation" was accepted by God as payment in full for our sins. By dying, Jesus defeated death—and so death is no longer our fate as the rightful punishment for rebelling against God. The risen Jesus can now offer us complete forgiveness and a whole new life as his glad and grateful servants.

The Bible verse for point 5 of *Two Ways to Live* reflects the joy of this truth:

> Praise be to the God and Father of our Lord Jesus Christ! In his great mercy he has given us new birth into a living hope through the resurrection of Jesus Christ from the dead... (1 Pet 1:3)[†]

The resurrection of Jesus means that the one who can forgive sins is alive! That's why we have a "living hope."

When the final judgment day comes, our future and salvation is assured—because the resurrected Jesus Christ will be there, ready and willing to forgive our sins on the basis of his atoning death and to grant us eternal life in his kingdom.

In the meantime, we experience something of that new life now. When we become a Christian, our old self is over and done with, crucified with Christ. We begin a new life under his rule, in his kingdom, living his way. We now belong to the resurrection age, the age to come; our citizenship is in heaven, and we eagerly await a savior from there who will return in glory to transform our lowly bodies to be like his glorious body (Phil 3:20-21).

In other words, the resurrection of Jesus changes the past, present, and future:

- He *has conquered death*—the resurrection shows that his sacrifice was acceptable to God, and that death no longer has power over us.
- He *now brings forgiveness and new life*—we can be restored to right relationship with God in our present experience, and begin a new life in his service.
- He *will return in glory*—the judgment day has been set and the judge appointed, and we look forward in hope and joy to that day coming, when evil and injustice will finally be swept away, and when his glorious eternal kingdom will be seen by all.

10. If we don't talk much about the resurrection in our gospel conversations, what might be the possible consequences? What might we leave out?

 **Alternatives**

*(Go to **matthiasmedia.com/learnthegospel** to watch bonus video 6b at this point, or read the following text aloud together.)*

a. Immortality of the soul

One common alternative to the idea of resurrection is the *immortality of the soul*—a very old teaching that has made a comeback in recent decades in the West through Eastern mysticism.

This is the idea that within us all there is a divine spark or drop of "world soul" that never dies, and that longs to return to its source. In some versions of this concept (such as reincarnation), the immortal part of the soul keeps on being recycled again and again until it finally escapes the prison of material existence and drops back into the big bucket of eternal soul. This is an awful idea. It means that we have no real personal identity, and that the ultimate goal for all of us is personal obliteration.

In Christianized versions of this teaching, the future we look forward to is not resurrection from the dead, but an escape from the body to a spiritualized heaven where we exist eternally as spirits. This has never been orthodox Christian teaching. The earliest Christian statements of belief (like the Apostles' Creed) look forward to "the resurrection of the body, and the life everlasting." The future hope is for a resurrected (or new) creation, filled with resurrected people and ruled by the resurrected Jesus Christ.

b. That resurrection is impossible

One of the standard objections to resurrection is that the very idea is implausible or ridiculous. Dead people simply do not rise from the dead.

This is a type of *a priori* argument—one that rules out in advance the claim that is being made, and thus will accept no evidence. But this sort of argument prevents us from ever discovering anything new. It's implausible and ridiculous, they once said, that the earth should revolve around the sun, or that black swans should exist. But then, by investigation and presentation of evidence, it was discovered that these things were not only possible but true.

It is certainly an extraordinary thing to claim that someone has risen from the dead. But if God is the all-powerful creator of all things, the one who brings every life into existence, then resurrection is hardly too difficult for him.

Related to this skepticism about the possibility of resurrection, it has been common over the centuries for people to produce various alternative explanations for the resurrection of Jesus: that he wasn't really dead, but swooning; that the disciples stole the body; and so on. None of these stands up to scrutiny. (For more on this, see *The Case for the Resurrection* by Gary Habermas and Michael Licona, or *Who Moved the Stone?* by Frank Morison.)

c. Spiritual resurrection

This is an alternative put forward mainly by unbelieving theologians who wish to retain "the resurrection" in name, but do not believe it. They argue that Jesus' resurrection was a spiritual or poetic event, not a physical one. This is a slightly desperate argument, and lacks any biblical evidence. In fact, 1 Corinthians 15 not only dispenses with the idea, but points out that if Jesus hasn't risen bodily from the dead then Christianity is pointless and we are still in our sins.

The New Testament goes to some trouble to show that Jesus' resurrection was not a mere spiritual projection, like a ghost. His resurrected body was a real body, capable of eating fish and able to be touched (Luke 24:41-42; John 20:24-29). It was a different sort of body—a body for the next age, a body capable of ascending to God's right hand—but a body all the same.

In other words, Jesus did not shed his humanity when

he died and rose from the dead. It's not as if "he went back to being God" after a brief excursion on earth. He rose *with a body*, and ascended with a body to sit on God's heavenly throne. That is, while being God's eternal Son, Jesus died as a real, flesh-and-blood human. He rose as a human with the kind of body we ourselves will possess in the new creation (see 1 Cor 15:35-57).

11. What objections to the resurrection of Jesus have you most commonly come across? How have you responded?

Summing up

Judgment, and salvation from judgment—this is the essence of the gospel of the crucified and risen Christ. In fact, this is what the apostles were commanded to preach as their gospel. Peter says so in Acts 10:

"And he commanded us to preach to the people and to testify that he is the one appointed by God to be judge of the living and the dead. To him all the prophets bear witness that everyone who believes in him receives forgiveness of sins through his name." (Acts 10:42-43)

Jesus is both the one who will judge the living and the dead and the who will save people from judgment on the basis of his atoning death.

It all hinges on his resurrection from the dead. As Paul himself says, if Christ was not raised, then our faith is futile and we are still in our sins (1 Cor 15:16-19).

One of the strengths of the *Two Ways to Live* outline is that it gives the resurrection of Jesus its full weight as an essential component of the New Testament gospel. It's an aspect of the gospel that many of us need to learn.

Before next time

Reflect and pray about what you've learned in this chapter

Look back over this chapter. Make notes in the margin about truths that prompt you to give thanks and pray. Spend some time thanking God and asking him to write these truths in your heart.

If you watched the videos in your group, make sure you read those sections of text—and vice versa (if you read aloud the sections of text, watch the relevant videos).

Learn point 6 of *Two Ways to Live*: Our response

Step 1

Read the statements aloud three times, tracing over the drawing as you do so.

> There are only two ways to live.

Our way

- reject God as ruler
  (draw humanity on left)
- live our own way
  (draw small crown)
- damaged by our rebellion
- facing death and judgment

God's new way

- submit to Jesus as our ruler
  (draw humanity on right)
- rely on Jesus' death and resurrection
  (draw large crown with J)
- forgiven by God
- receive a new life that lasts forever

Read the Bible verse and transition statement aloud three times.

> Whoever believes in the Son has eternal life, but whoever rejects the Son will not see life, for God's wrath remains on them. (John 3:36)†

> **So, which way do you want to live?**

Step 1a

Fill in the blanks in the statements.

There are _____.

Our way

- reject God _____
- live _____
- damaged by our rebellion
- facing _____ and _____

God's new way

- submit _____
  _____ ruler
- rely on Jesus' _____ and _____
- forgiven _____
- receive a new _____
  _____

Check your answers, and make any corrections. Read the corrected version of the statements aloud, doing the drawing as you go.

Fill in the blanks in the Bible verse and transition statement.

> Whoever _____ has eternal
> life, but whoever rejects the Son _____
> _____, for God's _____ them.
> (John 3:36)
>
> **So, which way _____?**

Check your answers, and make any corrections. Read the corrected Bible verse and transition statement aloud.

If possible, wait some time (perhaps even 24 hours) before moving on to step 2.

Step 2

Fill in the blanks in the statements.

_____ to live.

_____   **_____**

- _____   • _____ Jesus as
  ruler   _____

- _____ own way   • _____

- _____ our   death and resurrection
  rebellion   • _____ God

- _____   • _____
  judgment   _____ lasts forever

Check your answers, and make any corrections. Read the corrected version of the statements aloud, doing the drawing as you go.

Fill in the blanks in the Bible verse and transition statement.

> Whoever believes _____
>
> _____ , but _____
>
> _____ not see life, for God's wrath _____
>
> _____. (John ___:___)
>
> _____ , _____ **want to live?**

Check your answers, and make any corrections. Read the corrected Bible verse and transition statement aloud.

If possible, wait some time (perhaps even 24 hours) before moving on to step 3.

Step 3

On a blank sheet of paper, write out the statements from memory, and then correct your version.

Read the corrected statements aloud while doing the drawing.

Repeat this process until you can say the statements perfectly while doing the drawing.

On a blank sheet of paper, write out the Bible verse and transition statement, and then make any corrections.

Read the corrected version aloud.

Repeat the process until you can say the Bible verse and transition statement perfectly.

7. Our response

Review

In pairs or triplets, take it in turns to see if you can repeat to each other from memory *points 5 and 6* of *Two Ways to Live*, and reproduce the drawings.

The two ways to live

Points 1-5 of *Two Ways to Live* climax with the momentous news of the Christian gospel—so beautifully summarized by Paul as "Jesus Christ and him crucified" (1 Cor 2:2). Point 6 contains the response that news like this requires. It is the point where the extraordinary truths of the death and resurrection of Jesus confront me personally.

It is very important that we get to this point in our understanding and sharing of the gospel, because the gospel is the kind of message that demands a response.

Let's look at some examples of the response that the gospel calls for. Read through the following passages and note every instance of how people respond (or should respond) to the news about Jesus. (Underline the text, scribble in the margin—use some way of marking examples of "response" in these passages.)

> ¹⁴ Now after John was arrested, Jesus came into Galilee, proclaiming the gospel of God, ¹⁵ and saying, "The time is fulfilled, and the kingdom of God is at hand; repent and believe in the gospel." (Mark 1:14-15)

> ³⁶ [Peter finishing his sermon at Pentecost:] "Let all the house of Israel therefore know for certain that God has made him both Lord and Christ, this Jesus whom you crucified."

37 Now when they heard this they were cut to the heart, and said to Peter and the rest of the apostles, "Brothers, what shall we do?" 38 And Peter said to them, "Repent and be baptized every one of you in the name of Jesus Christ for the forgiveness of your sins, and you will receive the gift of the Holy Spirit." (Acts 2:36-38)

14 [Peter speaking to the crowd after healing the lame beggar:] "But you denied the Holy and Righteous One, and asked for a murderer to be granted to you, 15 and you killed the Author of life, whom God raised from the dead. To this we are witnesses. 16 And his name—by faith in his name—has made this man strong whom you see and know, and the faith that is through Jesus has given the man this perfect health in the presence of you all.

17 "And now, brothers, I know that you acted in ignorance, as did also your rulers. 18 But what God foretold by the mouth of all the prophets, that his Christ would suffer, he thus fulfilled. 19 Repent therefore, and turn back, that your sins may be blotted out, 20 that times of refreshing may come from the presence of the Lord, and that he may send the Christ appointed for you, Jesus, 21 whom heaven must receive until the time for restoring all the things about which God spoke by the mouth of his holy prophets long ago." (Acts 3:14-21)

[29] And the jailer called for lights and rushed in, and trembling with fear he fell down before Paul and Silas. [30] Then he brought them out and said, "Sirs, what must I do to be saved?" [31] And they said, "Believe in the Lord Jesus, and you will be saved, you and your household." [32] And they spoke the word of the Lord to him and to all who were in his house. [33] And he took them the same hour of the night and washed their wounds; and he was baptized at once, he and all his family. [34] Then he brought them up into his house and set food before them. And he rejoiced along with his entire household that he had believed in God. (Acts 16:29-34)

[18] [Paul speaking to the Ephesian elders:] "You yourselves know how I lived among you the whole time from the first day that I set foot in Asia, [19] serving the Lord with all humility and with tears and with trials that happened to me through the plots of the Jews; [20] how I did not shrink from declaring to you anything that was profitable, and teaching you in public and from house to house, [21] testifying both to Jews and to Greeks of repentance toward God and of faith in our Lord Jesus Christ." (Acts 20:18-21)

[8] For not only has the word of the Lord sounded forth from you in Macedonia and Achaia, but your

faith in God has gone forth everywhere, so that we need not say anything. [9] For they themselves report concerning us the kind of reception we had among you, and how you turned to God from idols to serve the living and true God, [10] and to wait for his Son from heaven, whom he raised from the dead, Jesus who delivers us from the wrath to come. (1 Thess 1:8-10)

1. Look back over what you've marked. How would you summarize the main aspects of the response that the gospel calls for?

2. What is it about the gospel message that leads to these responses?

The concepts you no doubt noticed cropping up repeatedly were "repent" or "repentance" and "believe" or "faith" (along with baptism). We'll look at these concepts further below, but it's worth noticing the stark and confronting nature of the choice that the gospel presents. We see it in the Bible verse that accompanies this final point of *Two Ways to Live*:

> Whoever believes in the Son has eternal life, but whoever rejects the Son will not see life, for God's wrath remains on him. (John 3:36)[†]

3. Look carefully at the alternatives outlined in John 3:36. What are the actions required in each case? Why do you think they are different? Or are they different?

4. Think back over what we've already learned in points 1-5 of *Two Ways to Live*. Where do you see the content of John 3:36 reflected in the various points of *Two Ways to Live*?

▶ The key concepts

*(Go to **matthiasmedia.com/learnthegospel** to watch bonus video 7a at this point, or read the following text aloud together.)*

In its diagnosis of our current position and the choice that is before us, the gospel has a binary logic to it. This is the sense in which there are only "two ways to live"—either to keep living our own way, or to make a decisive change and start living God's way.

We have already looked in some detail at what "our way" means in points 2 and 3 of *Two Ways to Live*. Point 6 summarizes that earlier material in four short statements:

Our way
- reject God as ruler
- live our own way
- damaged by our rebellion
- facing death and judgment

The outline then moves on to summarize God's new way—which includes the response that the gospel calls for and the promise of God to those who make such a response:

God's new way
- submit to Jesus as our ruler
- rely on Jesus' death and resurrection
- forgiven by God
- receive a new life that lasts forever

The response is to "submit" and "rely," and the blessings of forgiveness and new life are those that we've already looked at in point 5 (which flow from Jesus' resurrection).

These two words—"submit" and "rely"—are modern versions of the Bible words we saw repeatedly above: "repentance" and "faith."

a. Repentance

The average person thinks that "repentance" means feeling sorry for having done something—but this is not what repentance is really about. It is very possible to be deeply grieved about our actions, but to do nothing to change them. Second Corinthians 7 contains an example of this:

> As it is, I rejoice, not because you were grieved, but because you were grieved into repenting. For you felt a godly grief, so that you suffered no loss through us.
>
> For godly grief produces a repentance that leads to salvation without regret, whereas worldly grief produces death. (2 Cor 7:9-10)

Repentance is *a change of mind and will that issues in a change in action*. It means stopping in our tracks, turning 180 degrees, and starting off in a completely new direction. It's a "turnaround." Paul puts it beautifully in describing how the Thessalonians became Christians: "...you turned to God from idols to serve the living and true God, and to wait for his Son from heaven, whom he raised from the dead, Jesus who delivers us from the wrath to come" (1 Thess 1:9-10). Their conversion involved turning *to* God *from* idols, to serve the living and true God. Repentance always involves these two sides—turning away from something and turning towards something else.

Because the word "repentance" is so misunderstood in our society, we have not used it in the *Two Ways to Live* outline—although you may choose to do so as you share it with someone, depending on the context. We have chosen the word "submit," which is a fairly simple way of describing what happens when someone ceases a rebellion and turns back to live under the rightful authority of a ruler. They submit—in this case to Jesus as the ruler of the world.

b. Faith[3]

What then of faith? Faith is misunderstood in our society even more than repentance. Faith is not a religious experience or a feeling that some people have and some people don't. It is not a leap in the dark in the absence of evidence.

Put simply, faith is *trust*. It means to rely upon something, to depend upon it, to trust it. Faith is a common and

---

3   The word "faith" and the word "believe" are essentially the same in the Bible. They can have different nuances in English, but in the Bible "believe" is simply the verbal form of "faith." To "have faith" is to "believe."

universal human action, because we all depend or rely on certain things: on our parents, for example, or on our own wits, or on the chair that we're now sitting on. "Faith" is not a particularly religious or spiritual thing. It is simply trust.

Most people don't understand this. They say, "I don't have your faith" as if faith were a mysterious religious substance that some of us are blessed with and some of us have missed out on. Others think that faith as an object or action is complete in itself—that the important thing is simply to "have faith." But faith is only significant because of its *object*—because of the thing or person that we are trusting. If we replace the word "faith" with, say, the word "reliance," we can see the point. If I ask you, "Have you got reliance?" you would answer, "Reliance upon what?" And it is exactly the same with faith—faith is just the attitude or action of trusting in something. What is truly important is the thing or person that you trust in.

The response to the gospel in *Two Ways to Live* is to rely on or trust in Jesus, and in particular to rely on his saving death and resurrection. There was once a point when my trust was in myself, or in one of the false gods that I served. But having turned away from our rebellion, we now rely upon something different. We rely upon Jesus.

LEARN THE GOSPEL

5. The response to the gospel is twofold—to repent and believe (or have faith). What would the Christian life look like, do you think, if we didn't make both responses:

- if we trusted in Jesus but didn't repent?

- if we repented before God but didn't trust Jesus?

▶ Alternatives

*(Go to **matthiasmedia.com/learnthegospel** to watch bonus video 7b at this point, or read the following text aloud together.)*

a. Halfway

It is very common for people to resist the stark choice that the gospel confronts us with. After hearing *Two*

Ways to Live people will often say that they are currently "sort of in the middle." As they see it, sometimes they manage to do what God wants, and sometimes they go their own way. They don't think of themselves as rebels against God—they might be quite positive about him, and even go to church occasionally. But they recognize that they are by no means "living under God's rule."

The problem here is usually a faulty or incomplete understanding of sin (point 2). They think that sin is really breaking certain rules, and that Christianity is about getting better at keeping the rules (and thereby being acceptable to God). They may even think that the goal is to get above 50% and so get a "pass" and be let into heaven.

But (as we saw earlier) sin is not just about individual acts but our whole relationship with God. It's about our consistent and persistent declaration of independence from God—seeking to live our own lives our own way, to be the captains of our own souls. Whether our rebellion takes the form of gross immorality or religious morality, we are all still rebels at heart, alienated from God and in need of forgiveness.

This is the underlying problem. And once we have understood that, and understood what God has done about that through the Lord Jesus Christ, we can begin to grasp why the required response is to turn back from our rebellion and submit in faith to Jesus.

b. Our contribution

It is difficult for self-centered people like us to believe that there is nothing we have to contribute in order to be acceptable to God. Surely some religious activities are required, like going to church or mass, or giving up ice cream for Lent.

But there is nothing that a rebel can do to stop being a rebel except turn around and submit. And there is nothing that he can do to atone for his past rebellion—since by submitting to the government he is only doing what he should have been doing all along. He is not earning extra merit, but simply doing what was always his duty.

So there is nothing to contribute. Jesus has done it all by dying and rising again to bring us forgiveness and new life.

c. Friend but not lord

One common alternative is to preach a gospel that offers people forgiveness and friendship with Jesus, but does not mention his lordship—as if his lordship is a bonus extra that you can come to terms with later.

But you can't cease rebellion against a ruler without submitting to that ruler. You can't enter God's kingdom without bowing to God's king. True, you can't enter that kingdom until your rebellion has been forgiven, but the very act of turning from our rebellion against God involves (by definition) a turning to Jesus as our king and ruler.

We can't be saved by Jesus unless he truly is the risen, conquering lord. And if he is the lord, then we must bow before him in submission and obedience. It's not possible to have Jesus as our savior now and as our lord at some later point. The nature of repentance and faith is to turn back and submit in trust to Jesus as the crucified king.

6. Why do you think religious or morally upright people often find the gospel difficult to accept?

Summing up

This final point of *Two Ways to Live* calls for the response that the previous five points have been working towards.

If we are rebels against our creator, and deserving of his judgment, and if that creator has sent his Son into the world to take the punishment for that rebellion, and to be raised up as the ruler and judge of all—then there is only one thing we can do: we must cease our rebellion and submit to the ruler, to Jesus, God's Son.

And we can only be forgiven the punishment that is

due to us (because of our rebellion) through his death on our behalf. We have no option but to trust entirely in him for the forgiveness that we so desperately need.

In each case, the choice is binary. Remain a rebel or repent. Remain under God's judgment or trust in Jesus for forgiveness.

There are only two ways to live.

Before next time

a. Reflect and pray about what you've learned in this chapter

Look back over this chapter. Make notes in the margin about truths that prompt you to give thanks and pray. Spend some time thanking God and asking him to write these truths in your heart.

If you watched the videos in your group, make sure you read those sections of text—and vice versa (if you read aloud the sections of text, watch the relevant videos).

b. Revise the whole *Two Ways to Live* outline

In our next and final session, we're going to present to each other the whole *Two Ways to Live* outline from memory. So use this week to revise all six points of the outline and the drawings.

8. Building on the foundation

Review

In the whole group, or in groups of four, take it in turns to present from memory the whole *Two Ways to Live* outline to one another, including the drawings:

Let's also review what we've learned about the gospel by talking about the connections between the various points of the *Two Ways to Live* outline.

1. How do each of the ideas in box 2 depend on what is established in box 1? Try to explain the connection in each case.

2. Imagine that we blanked out box 3, and went straight from "sin" (box 2) to "Jesus' death" (box 4). See if you can come up with a clear and coherent explanation of Jesus' death without referring to any of the concepts in box 3.

3. What connections do you see between box 5 and:

- box 1?

- box 3?

- box 4?

4. Thinking back over the material we've covered together, what have you learned about the gospel that was new to you or was particularly striking or challenging?

The gospel-shaped life

We began this course on learning the gospel by talking about how important it is to lay down true and solid foundations for the Christian life. God willing, that's what we've now done by clearly and thoroughly understanding the gospel.

But although foundations are vital and will determine the shape and solidity of the building, getting the foundations right is just the beginning of the project. Foundations are meant to be built on.

That's what we're going to think about in this final chapter. Now that we (hopefully!) understand the gospel more clearly, *how does the gospel of Jesus' death and resurrection form the ongoing basis of our Christian lives?* What sort of gospel-shaped building should we be constructing?

Fortunately, the letters of the New Testament are full of advice on this question. In fact, the striking thing about the Epistles is just how consistently the apostles turn back to the fundamental truths of the gospel in order to encourage and correct and exhort their readers to live the Christian life, in whatever issue or situation they are discussing. We could turn to almost any of the New Testament letters for examples of this, but we're going to zero in on the first letter of Peter and learn its lessons about how to live in light of the gospel of the crucified and risen Lord Jesus Christ.

Let's dive into Peter's first chapter, focusing on verses 3-9 and 13-21 (we'll come back to verses 10-12 soon). As you read, underline everything that has <u>already been done</u> for Peter's readers in the past with a single line, everything that is <u>happening now</u> in their present experience with a double line, and everything that <u>relates to the future</u> with a wavy line.

> [3] Blessed be the God and Father of our Lord Jesus Christ! According to his great mercy, he has caused us to be born again to a living hope through the resurrection of Jesus Christ from the dead, [4] to an inheritance that is imperishable, undefiled, and unfading, kept in heaven for you, [5] who by God's power are being guarded through faith for a salvation ready to be revealed in the last time. [6] In this you rejoice, though now for a little while, if necessary, you have been grieved by various trials, [7] so that the tested genuineness of your faith— more precious than gold that perishes though it is tested by fire—may be found to result in praise and glory and honor at the revelation of Jesus Christ. [8] Though you have not seen him, you love him. Though you do not now see him, you believe in him and rejoice with joy that is inexpressible and filled with glory, [9] obtaining the outcome of your faith, the salvation of your souls.
>
> ...

¹³ Therefore, preparing your minds for action, and being sober-minded, set your hope fully on the grace that will be brought to you at the revelation of Jesus Christ. ¹⁴ As obedient children, do not be conformed to the passions of your former ignorance, ¹⁵ but as he who called you is holy, you also be holy in all your conduct, ¹⁶ since it is written, "You shall be holy, for I am holy." ¹⁷ And if you call on him as Father who judges impartially according to each one's deeds, conduct yourselves with fear throughout the time of your exile, ¹⁸ knowing that you were ransomed from the futile ways inherited from your forefathers, not with perishable things such as silver or gold, ¹⁹ but with the precious blood of Christ, like that of a lamb without blemish or spot. ²⁰ He was foreknown before the foundation of the world but was made manifest in the last times for the sake of you ²¹ who through him are believers in God, who raised him from the dead and gave him glory, so that your faith and hope are in God. (1 Pet 1:3-21)

5. How would you summarize (in a sentence or two) from these verses:

- what has already happened in the past or been done for them?

- their present experience?

- what they are expecting or hoping for in the future?

6. Which do you think is more important for shaping and directing their present lives: the future or the past? What arguments would you make on each side?

Now let's read the bit we missed out earlier:

> ¹⁰ Concerning this salvation, the prophets who prophesied about the grace that was to be yours searched and inquired carefully, ¹¹ inquiring what person or time the Spirit of Christ in them was indicating when he predicted the sufferings of Christ and the subsequent glories. ¹² It was revealed to them that they were serving not themselves but you, in the things that have now been announced to you through those who preached the good news to you by the Holy Spirit sent from heaven, things into which angels long to look. (1 Pet 1:10-12)

This is a complicated couple of sentences, but the heart of it is in verse 11. The events that the prophets predicted (without fully understanding them) were *"the sufferings of Christ and the subsequent glories."* And the prophets' predictions were fulfilled in the "things that [were] announced" to Peter's readers, the gospel that was preached to them.

So the gospel that was preached was about "the sufferings of Christ and the subsequent glories." It was about Christ ransoming them from the futile ways of their fathers through his blood (vv. 18-19), and then rising to life and glory (v. 21). In *Two Ways to Live* terms, it was point 4 followed by point 5.

Peter's overall point is that *the Christian life of his readers has this same shape.*

7. Look briefly back over your responses to verses 3-9 and 13-21. Where do you see:

- the difficulties, sufferings or challenges that Christians face now in their lives?

- the future or "subsequent" glories that Christians look forward to in hope?

Now let's look at two other passages in 1 Peter that show how the gospel shapes our lives as Christians.

¹⁸ Servants, be subject to your masters with all respect, not only to the good and gentle but also to the unjust. ¹⁹ For this is a gracious thing, when, mindful of God, one endures sorrows while suffering unjustly. ²⁰ For what credit is it if, when you sin and are beaten for it, you endure? But if when you do good and suffer for it you endure, this is a gracious thing in the sight of God. ²¹ For

to this you have been called, because Christ also suffered for you, leaving you an example, so that you might follow in his steps. [22] He committed no sin, neither was deceit found in his mouth. [23] When he was reviled, he did not revile in return; when he suffered, he did not threaten, but continued entrusting himself to him who judges justly. [24] He himself bore our sins in his body on the tree, that we might die to sin and live to righteousness. By his wounds you have been healed. (1 Pet 2:18-24)

8. What aspect of the gospel is being referred to in this passage?

9. Where would it fit (if at all) in the *Two Ways to Live* framework?

10. What implication or application does this aspect of the gospel have for the Christian life?

^{13} Now who is there to harm you if you are zealous for what is good? ^{14} But even if you should suffer for righteousness' sake, you will be blessed. Have no fear of them, nor be troubled, ^{15} but in your hearts honor Christ the Lord as holy, always being prepared to make a defense to anyone who asks you for a reason for the hope that is in you; yet do it with gentleness and respect, ^{16} having a good conscience, so that, when you are slandered, those who revile your good behavior in Christ may be put to shame. ^{17} For it is better to suffer for doing good, if that should be God's will, than for doing evil.

^{18} For Christ also suffered once for sins, the righteous for the unrighteous, that he might bring us to God, being put to death in the flesh but made alive in the spirit... (1 Pet 3:13-18)

11. What aspect of the gospel is being referred to in this passage?

12. Where would it fit (if at all) in the *Two Ways to Live* framework?

13. What implication or application does this aspect of the gospel have for the Christian life?

▶ The key concepts

*(Go to **matthiasmedia.com/learnthegospel** to watch bonus video 8 at this point, or read the following text aloud together.)*

The gospel is the foundation of our Christian lives because it proclaims the death of our old self on the cross with Christ, and the beginning of a completely new, forgiven life under his lordship. This was the message of those extraordinary verses in 2 Corinthians 5 (which we looked at chapter 5):

> For the love of Christ controls us, because we
> have concluded this: that one has died for all,
> therefore all have died; and he died for all, that
> those who live might no longer live for themselves
> but for him who for their sake died and was raised.
> (2 Cor 5:14-15)

The change that the gospel brings is decisive and complete. As Paul says a couple of verses later: "Therefore, if anyone is in Christ, he is a new creation. The old has passed away; behold, the new has come" (2 Cor 5:17).

But the implications of this profound change continue to be worked out in our lives every day—because the remains of our old life linger with us. We retain an urge to put that little crown back on our heads. We confront stubbornly sinful habits and thoughts and attitudes that need killing off. There is an ongoing battle between that old part of us (which the Bible often calls "the flesh") and the new life we live in the Spirit. This is how Paul puts it in Colossians:

> If then you have been raised with Christ, seek the things that are above, where Christ is, seated at the right hand of God. Set your minds on things that are above, not on things that are on earth. For you have died, and your life is hidden with Christ in God. When Christ who is your life appears, then you also will appear with him in glory.
>
> Put to death therefore what is earthly in you: sexual immorality, impurity, passion, evil desire, and covetousness, which is idolatry. (Col 3:1-5)

It's as if we need to go back to point 4 of *Two Ways to Live* every day and to keep nailing the old sinful part of ourselves to the cross—to remind ourselves that we have died, and that our new life in point 5 has begun.

The passages we looked at above in 1 Peter also see our Christian lives as being lived in points 4 and 5 of the outline, but in a slightly different way. Just as Christ passed through suffering and death into the glory of the resurrection and his eternal place at God's right hand, so our Christian lives have a similar shape. We experience the sufferings and trials of life now in a sinful world, and look forward with certainty and assurance to the resurrection of our bodies and the life everlasting.

When we experience suffering, trials, and unjust

treatment for doing the right thing, we shouldn't be surprised, says Peter. This is what Jesus also endured, all the way to the cross. The more our hearts are full of the gospel of the suffering, dying, resurrected Christ, the more we will understand the trials of our present experience, and the more we will endure them with trust and hope.

Peter also says that a heart full of the gospel will always be ready to *speak about the gospel to others* (1 Pet 3:15-16). There's a Christ-focused reason for speaking (because in our hearts we know that Christ is lord of all), and a Christ-like manner of speaking (with gentleness and respect). Peter's assumption is that living faithfully with Christ as lord will provide opportunities for speaking about our hope. Paul says much the same when he urges the Colossians to make the most of their opportunities to speak to outsiders in the context of everyday life (Col 4:5-6).

But while (in one sense) sharing the wonderful news of the gospel with others seems the only and obvious thing to do, we also shouldn't be surprised that we find it challenging, nor should we be surprised that ridicule or suffering might follow. When we join with Christ, our path will be the same as his: doing what is good (in this case, speaking the gospel well); and experiencing unjust suffering for it, to be followed in the end by vindication and glory.

14. Think back over the *Two Ways to Live* gospel framework that we have learned. Can you think of ways in which it has challenged or encouraged or rebuked you in your Christian life?

15. What reasons or motivations can you see for sharing the gospel from:

- point 1 of *Two Ways to Live*?

- points 2-3?

- point 4?

- point 5?

16. What challenges you or scares you about sharing the gospel with others?

Where to from here?

At one level, the follow-up to this course is the rest of your life. As we've seen above, the gospel not only starts the Christian life; it drives and shapes it. The gospel constantly assures us of our forgiven status before God (on the basis of Jesus' atoning death) and exhorts us to conform our lives more and more to the risen Jesus Christ, the lord of all. The gospel is the center and foundation, and the engine that drives Christian growth and maturity.

It's also a message that begs to be shared with others. Thanks to this course, we now know that gospel much more clearly and thoroughly.

But *knowing* the gospel is one thing; *sharing* it naturally and easily in our everyday conversations with friends is another. That requires some further thought. In fact, that's how the *Two Ways to Live* outline first came to be written—as a tool for helping Christians articulate their faith to others in everyday conversation. There's a separate training resource designed to help you learn to do exactly that. It's called *Share the Gospel*. It starts with the gospel outline you've learned, then goes on to explore:

- how to adapt and flesh out the outline according to your own style of speech and conversation
- how to have gospel conversations from multiple different starting points
- how to answer questions (and lead from questions into talking about the heart of the gospel)
- how to help someone respond to the gospel
- the place of prayer in evangelism
- and more.

See **matthiasmedia.com/sharethegospel** for more details about how to be trained with *Share the Gospel*.

Let's conclude with thanksgiving and prayer:

- Give thanks for the glories of the gospel, and for the different aspects of the gospel that you've learned about in this book.

- Pray for one another that the gospel would shape and determine and drive our lives. Pray about some specific aspects of Christian living that you've been challenged about.
- Pray that we would not keep the gospel knowledge we've learned to ourselves, but that we would work at sharing it with others.

Feedback on this resource

We really appreciate getting feedback about our resources—not just suggestions for how to improve them, but also positive feedback and ways they can be used. We especially love to hear that the resources may have helped someone in their Christian growth.

You can send feedback to us via the 'Feedback' menu in our online store, or write to us at info@matthiasmedia.com.au.

Appendix: Suggested timings

Chapter	Section	Timing	Section	Timing	Section	Timing	Sec
1	Intro	10	First importance	10	The courier and his message	10	More go reasons the gos
2	Review	6	The place to start	22	The key concepts	14	Alternat
3	Review	6	The story of sin	22	The key concepts	14	Alternat
4	Review	6	The God who judges	22	The key concepts	16	Alternat
5	Review	10	The crux of the gospel	20	The key concepts	18	A comm alternat
6	Review	8	The essential resurrection	22	The key concepts	12	Alternat
7	Review	8	The two ways to live	22	The key concepts	14	Alternat
8	Review	16	The gospel-shaped life	22	The key concepts	14	Where t here?

Section	Timing	Section	Timing	Section	Timing	Total time (mins)
The engine of growth and the word that we share	10	How we'll learn the gospel	4	Before next time	4	**60**
Summing up	2	Before next time	2			**60**
Summing up	2	Before next time	2			**60**
Summing up	2	Before next time	2			**60**
Summing up	2	Before next time	2			**60**
Summing up	2	Before next time	2			**60**
Summing up	2	Before next time	2			**60**
						60

❀matthiasmedia

Matthias Media is an evangelical publishing ministry that seeks to persuade all Christians of the truth of God's purposes in Jesus Christ as revealed in the Bible, and equip them with high-quality resources, so that by the work of the Holy Spirit they will:

- abandon their lives to the honour and service of Christ in daily holiness and decision-making
- pray constantly in Christ's name for the fruitfulness and growth of his gospel
- speak the Bible's life-changing word whenever and however they can—in the home, in the world and in the fellowship of his people.

Our wide range of resources includes Bible studies, books, training courses, tracts and children's material. To find out more, and to access samples and free downloads, visit our website:

www.matthiasmedia.com

How to buy our resources

1. Direct from us over the internet:
   – in the US: www.matthiasmedia.com
   – in Australia: www.matthiasmedia.com.au

2. Direct from us by phone: please visit our website for current phone contact information.

3. Through a range of outlets in various parts of the world. Visit **www.matthiasmedia.com/contact** for details about recommended retailers in your part of the world.

4. Trade enquiries can be addressed to:
   – in the US and Canada: sales@matthiasmedia.com
   – in Australia and the rest of the world: sales@matthiasmedia.com.au

Register at our website for our **free** regular email update to receive information about the latest new resources, **exclusive special offers**, and free articles to help you grow in your Christian life and ministry.

Two Ways to Live

two ways to live

Two Ways to Live is a simple, clear, and challenging outline of the Christian gospel. It explains the message of Jesus Christ in the context of the overarching story of the Bible, giving the non-Christian hearer or reader all the presuppositions and assumptions they need to grasp the real significance of Jesus' death and resurrection. In other words, it is a brief and logical presentation that still provides all the foundations a non-Christian needs to know in order to become a Christian.

Updated in 2021 with revised text and refreshed graphics, every church and individual should have copies ready to share.

FOR MORE INFORMATION OR TO ORDER CONTACT:

Matthias Media
mail: sales@matthiasmedia.com.au
www.matthiasmedia.com.au

Matthias Media (USA)
Email: sales@matthiasmedia.com
www.matthiasmedia.com

Two Ways to Live

① GOD, THE GOOD RULER AND CREATOR

- God is the ruler of the world.
- He made the world.
- He made us to rule his good world, giving thanks and honor to him.

You are worthy, our Lord and God, to receive glory and honor and power, for you created all things, and by your will they were created and have their being. (Revelation 4:11)†

This is how God created things to be. But it's fairly obvious that this is not our experience of the world now. What happened?

② OUR REBELLION AGAINST GOD

- We all reject God as our ruler by running our own lives our own way.
- By rebelling against God's way, we damage ourselves, each other, and the world.

We all, like sheep, have gone astray, each of us has turned to our own way... (Isaiah 53:6a)†

The question is: what will God do about our rebellion against him?

③ GOD'S JUSTICE

- God won't let us rebel against him forever.
- God's punishment for rebellion is death and judgment.

Just as people are destined to die once, and after that to face judgment... (Hebrews 9:27)†

This is hard to hear. It means that we are all in deep trouble. But it's not the end of the story.

④ GOD SENT JESUS TO DIE FOR US

- Because of his love, God sent his Son into the world: the man Jesus Christ.
- Jesus always lived under God's rule.
- But Jesus took our punishment by dying in our place.

We all, like sheep, have gone astray, each of us has turned to our own way; and the LORD has laid on him the iniquity of us all. (Isaiah 53:6)†

But that's not all.

⑤ JESUS, THE RISEN RULER AND SAVIOR

- God raised Jesus to life again as the ruler and judge of the world.
- Jesus has conquered death, now brings forgiveness and new life, and will return in glory.

Praise be to the God and Father of our Lord Jesus Christ! In his great mercy he has given us new birth into a living hope through the resurrection of Jesus Christ from the dead... (1 Peter 1:3)†

Well, where does that leave us? It leaves us with a clear choice between two ways to live.

⑥ TWO WAYS TO LIVE

There are only two ways to live.

Our way
- reject God as ruler
- live our own way
- damaged by our rebellion
- facing death and judgment

God's new way
- submit to Jesus as our ruler
- rely on Jesus' death and resurrection
- forgiven by God
- receive a new life that lasts forever

Whoever believes in the Son has eternal life, but whoever rejects the Son will not see life, for God's wrath remains on them. (John 3:36)†

So, which way do you want to live?